Geolocation in iOS

Alasdair Allan

O'REILLY®

Beijing · Cambridge · Farnham · Köln · Sebastopol · Tokyo

Geolocation in iOS
by Alasdair Allan

Published by O'Reilly Media, Inc., 1005 Gravenstein Highway North, Sebastopol, CA 95472.

O'Reilly books may be purchased for educational, business, or sales promotional use. Online editions are also available for most titles (*http://my.safaribooksonline.com*). For more information, contact our corporate/institutional sales department: 800-998-9938 or *corporate@oreilly.com*.

Editors: Shawn Wallace and Brian Jepson	**Cover Designer:** Karen Montgomery
Production Editor: Kara Ebrahim	**Interior Designer:** David Futato
Proofreader: Kara Ebrahim	**Illustrator:** Rebecca Demarest

October 2012:   First Edition.

Revision History for the First Edition:
    2012-10-01   First release
See *http://oreilly.com/catalog/errata.csp?isbn=9781449308445* for release details.

ISBN: 978-1-449-30844-5

[LSI]

1349100352

Table of Contents

Preface

The mobile phone—specifically the iPhone, which continues to define the state of the art for smartphones—has become the primary interface device for geographically-tagged data.

Who Should Read This Book?

This book provides an introduction to the hot topic of location on the iOS platform. If you are a programmer who has had some experience with iOS before, this book will help you push your knowledge further. If you are an experienced Mac programmer and are already familiar with Objective-C as a language, this book will dive deeper into Core Location and Map Kit, as well as some of the more important third-party tools, to give you a close look at the geolocation capabilities of the iOS platform.

What Should You Already Know?

This book assumes some previous experience with the Objective-C language. Additionally, some familiarity with the iOS platform would be helpful. If you're new to the iOS platform you may be interested in *Learning iOS Programming* (*http://shop.oreilly.com/product/0636920018490.do*), also by Alasdair Allan (O'Reilly).

What Will You Learn?

This book will guide you through developing applications for the iOS platform. These applications make use of the onboard sensors and geolocation capabilities of the device in your hands to give you the background and skills to build your own applications using the hottest location-aware technology for any mobile platform.

What's In This Book?

Chapter 1

> This chapter summarizes the available sensors on the iPhone and iPad platforms and how they could be used in applications. It talks about the differences between the hardware platforms.

Chapter 2

> This chapter includes a discussion on the Core Location framework, covering standard location monitoring as well as the significant-change location service, which provides a low-power way to get the current location and be notified of changes to that location. It also covers region monitoring, which provides geofencing capabilities on the platform.

Chapter 3

> This chapter includes a discussion on the MapKit framework, which allows you to embed maps directly into your application's views, and provides support for annotating these maps.

Chapter 4

> This chapter shows how to use the onboard magnetometer, which is present in many iOS devices, as a digital compass using the Core Location framework.

Chapter 5

> This chapter discusses the geocoding capabilities of the platform that allow you to go from a latitude and longitude to a place name, and vice versa.

Chapter 6

> This chapter walks through code that allows you to display heat maps on top of a standard Map Kit view.

Chapter 7

> This chapter points to more information and some of the available third-party *software development kits* (SDKs) that make it easier to carry out geocoding, geofencing, and real-time location streaming as part of your application.

Conventions Used in This Book

The following typographical conventions are used in this book:

Italic

> Indicates new terms, URLs, email addresses, filenames, and file extensions.

`Constant width`

> Used for program listings, as well as within paragraphs to refer to program elements such as variable or function names, databases, data types, environment variables, statements, and keywords.

Constant width bold

> Shows commands or other text that should be typed literally by the user.

Constant width italic

> Shows text that should be replaced with user-supplied values or by values determined by context.

 This icon signifies a tip, suggestion, or general note.

 This icon signifies a warning or caution.

Using Code Examples

This book is here to help you get your job done. In general, you may use the code in this book in your programs and documentation. You do not need to contact us for permission unless you're reproducing a significant portion of the code. For example, writing a program that uses several chunks of code from this book does not require permission. Selling or distributing a CD-ROM of examples from O'Reilly books does require permission. Answering a question by citing this book and quoting example code does not require permission. Incorporating a significant amount of example code from this book into your product's documentation does require permission.

We appreciate, but do not require, attribution. An attribution usually includes the title, author, publisher, and ISBN. For example: "*Geolocation in iOS*, by Alasdair Allan. Copyright 2012 O'Reilly Media, Inc., ISBN 978-1-4493-0844-5."

If you feel your use of code examples falls outside fair use or the permission given here, feel free to contact us at *permissions@oreilly.com*.

Safari® Books Online

 Safari Books Online (*www.safaribooksonline.com*) is an on-demand digital library that delivers expert content in both book and video form from the world's leading authors in technology and business.

Technology professionals, software developers, web designers, and business and creative professionals use Safari Books Online as their primary resource for research, problem solving, learning, and certification training.

Safari Books Online offers a range of product mixes and pricing programs for organizations, government agencies, and individuals. Subscribers have access to thousands of books, training videos, and prepublication manuscripts in one fully searchable database from publishers like O'Reilly Media, Prentice Hall Professional, Addison-Wesley Professional, Microsoft Press, Sams, Que, Peachpit Press, Focal Press, Cisco Press, John Wiley & Sons, Syngress, Morgan Kaufmann, IBM Redbooks, Packt, Adobe Press, FT Press, Apress, Manning, New Riders, McGraw-Hill, Jones & Bartlett, Course Technology, and dozens more. For more information about Safari Books Online, please visit us online.

How to Contact Us

Please address comments and questions concerning this book to the publisher:

> O'Reilly Media, Inc.
> 1005 Gravenstein Highway North
> Sebastopol, CA 95472
> 800-998-9938 (in the United States or Canada)
> 707-829-0515 (international or local)
> 707-829-0104 (fax)

We have a web page for this book, where we list errata, examples, and any additional information. You can access this page at *http://oreil.ly/geolocation-ios*. Supplementary materials are also available at *http://www.programmingiphonesensors.com/*.

To comment or ask technical questions about this book, send email to *bookquestions@oreilly.com*.

For more information about our books, courses, conferences, and news, see our website at *http://www.oreilly.com*.

Find us on Facebook: *http://facebook.com/oreilly*

Follow us on Twitter: *http://twitter.com/oreillymedia*

Watch us on YouTube: *http://www.youtube.com/oreillymedia*

Acknowledgments

Everyone has one book in them. This isn't it; it's my fifth, and hopefully not my last by any means. Nonetheless, they don't really get much easier to write. I'd therefore like to thank my editors Brian Jepson and Shawn Wallace for prodding and poking until I actually finally set some of this material down in print. I'd also like to thank my long-suffering wife, Gemma Hobson. I'm not entirely sure why she lets me keep writing; it's almost certainly nothing to do with the royalty checks. Finally, to my son Alex, who is still young enough that he's not entirely sure what daddy is doing. Sorry for being so grumpy while I went about this whole business one more time.

CHAPTER 1

Introduction

The arrival of the iPhone changed the whole direction of software development for mobile platforms, and has had a profound impact on the hardware design of the smartphones that have followed it. The arrival of the iPad has turned what was a single class of devices into a platform.

That platform is one of the most popular for geolocation: it's used for everything from driving directions to finding a restaurant. As a developer, you can get in on the geolocation game by using the Core Location framework, one of the most powerful and interesting frameworks in the iOS SDK. It abstracts the details of determining a user's location, and does all the heavy lifting for you behind the scenes.

Hardware Support

Unique amongst modern mobile platforms, Apple has gone to great lengths to ensure that your code will run on all of the current iOS-based devices. Yet despite this, there is still some variation in hardware between the various models (see Table 1-1).

Table 1-1. Hardware support in various iPhone, iPod touch, and iPad models

Hardware features	iPhone					iPod touch				iPad		iPad 2		New iPad	
	Original	3G	3GS	4	4s	1st gen	2nd gen	3rd gen	4th gen	WiFi	3G	WiFi	3G	WiFi	3G
Cellular	✓	✓	✓	✓	✓	✗	✗	✗	✗	✗	✓	✓	✓	✓	✓
WiFi	✓	✓	✓	✓	✓	✓	✓	✓	✓	✓	✓	✓	✓	✓	✓
Bluetooth	✓	✓	✓	✓	✓	✗	✓	✓	✓	✓	✓	✓	✓	✓	✓
Speaker	✓	✓	✓	✓	✓	✗	✓	✓	✓	✓	✓	✓	✓	✓	✓
Audio In	✓	✓	✓	✓	✓	✗	✓	✓	✓	✓	✓	✓	✓	✓	✓
Accelerometer	✓	✓	✓	✓	✓	✓	✓	✓	✓	✓	✓	✓	✓	✓	✓

Hardware features	iPhone					iPod touch				iPad		iPad 2		New iPad	
	Original	3G	3GS	4	4s	1st gen	2nd gen	3rd gen	4th gen	WiFi	3G	WiFi	3G	WiFi	3G
Magnetometer	✗	✗	✓	✓	✓	✗	✗	✗	✗	✓	✓	✓	✓	✓	✓
Gyroscope	✗	✗	✗	✓	✓	✗	✗	✗	✓	✗	✗	✓	✓	✓	✓
GPS	✗	✓	✓	✓	✓	✗	✗	✗	✗	✗	✓	✗	✓	✗	✓
Proximity Sensor	✓	✓	✓	✓	✓	✗	✗	✗	✗	✗	✗	✗	✗	✗	✗
Camera	✓	✓	✓	✓	✓	✗	✗	✗	✓	✗	✗	✓	✓	✓	✓
Video	✗	✗	✓	✓	✓	✗	✗	✗	✓	✗	✗	✓	✓	✓	✓
Vibration	✓	✓	✓	✓	✓	✗	✗	✗	✗	✗	✗	✗	✗	✗	✗
Retina Display	✗	✗	✗	✓	✓	✗	✗	✗	✓	✗	✗	✗	✗	✓	✓

Detecting Hardware Differences

Because your application will likely support multiple devices, you'll need to write code to check which features are supported and adjust your application's behavior as appropriate.

GPS Availability

The short answer to a fairly commonly asked question is that, unfortunately, the Core Location framework does not provide any way to get direct information about the availability of specific hardware such as the GPS at application run time, although you can check whether location services are enabled:

```
BOOL locationAvailable = [CLLocationManager locationServicesEnabled];
```

However, while you cannot check for the availability of GPS using Core Location from your application, you can require the presence of GPS hardware for your application to load (see "Setting Required Hardware Capabilities" on page 3).

Compass Availability

Fortunately, Core Location does allow you to check for the presence of the magnetometer (digital compass) fairly simply in your application:

```
BOOL magnetometerAvailable = [CLLocationManager headingAvailable];
```

Setting Required Hardware Capabilities

If your application requires specific hardware features in order to run you can add a list of required capabilities to your application's *Info.plist* file. Your application will not start unless those capabilities are present on the device.

To do this, open your project and then click your application's *Info.plist* file to open it in the Xcode editor. Click the last entry in the list and a + button will appear on the right side of the key-value pair table.

Click this button to add a new row to the table, and scroll down the list of possible options and select "Required device capabilities" (the `UIRequiredDeviceCapabilities` key). This will add an (empty) array to the *plist* file.

The allowed values for the keys are:

```
telephony
wifi
sms
still-camera
auto-focus-camera
front-facing-camera
camera-flash
video-camera
accelerometer
gyroscope
location-services
gps
magnetometer
gamekit
microphone
opengles-1
opengles-2
armv6
armv7
peer-peer
bluetooth-le
```

A full description of the possible keys is given in the Device Support section of the iOS Application Programming Guide available from the iOS Development Center.

Background Modes

Setting the `UIBackgroundModes` key in the Application's *Info.plist* file notifies the operating systems that the application should continue to run in the background, even after the user closes it, since it provides specific background services.

Regarding background modes, Apple says: "These keys should be used sparingly and only by applications providing the indicated services. Where alternatives for running in the background exist, those alternatives should be used instead. For example, applications can use the significant location change interface to receive location events instead of registering as a background location application."

There are three possible key values: *audio*, *location*, and *voip*. In this book, you'll be most interested in the location key, which indicates that the application provides location-based information for the user using the standard Core Location services, rather than the newer significant location change service, and should continue to do so in the background (see Chapter 2).

CHAPTER 2

Core Location

Core Location can provide the latitude, longitude, and altitude of the user's device, along with the level of accuracy to which this information is known, and the direction in which the device is moving. If a magnetometer is present, the framework can also return the device heading and the accuracy to which that is known.

The Standard Location Service

The Core Location framework is an abstraction layer on top of three main methods of geolocation:

1. The least accurate level uses the cell network to locate the user (the process is similar to triangulation but more complex). This can quickly provide a position to around 12 km accuracy, which can be reduced to 2–3 km after some time, depending on the tower density at your current location.

2. The next accuracy level is obtained by utilizing a WiFi-based positioning system. This is much more precise, giving a position to approximately 100 m. However, it requires the user to be in range of a wireless hotspot that is tracked by the system.

3. Finally, the highest level of accuracy is obtained by using GPS hardware, if present, which should provide a position to less than 40 m.

Since the framework is intended to abstract both the user and the developer from the hardware layer, it—perhaps unfortunately—does not provide any way to get direct information about the availability of specific hardware (for instance, the availability of GPS).

Therefore, as a developer the only control you have over which method is used to determine the user's location is through the level of accuracy you request, although the actual accuracy achieved is not guaranteed.

However, this can be an advantage. Because the hardware is abstracted away from your code, you don't have to worry about the introduction of new devices. Perhaps the next iPhone or iPad device might come with support for the European Galileo or Russian

GLONASS positioning systems. If so, you don't have to worry about that; the Core Location framework will take care of it for you behind the scenes.

 Some users may choose to explicitly disable reporting of their position. You should therefore always check to see whether location services are enabled before attempting to turn on these services. This will avoid unnecessary prompting from your application.

Basic Usage

The Core Location framework is implemented using the CLLocationManager class. The following code will create an instance of this class. As Core Location is event-based, it will send location update messages to the designated delegate class when a new location becomes available.

```
CLLocationManager *locationManager = [[CLLocationManager alloc] init];
locationManager.delegate = self;
if ([CLLocationManager locationServicesEnabled] ) {
    [locationManager startUpdatingLocation];
} else {
    NSLog(@"Location services not enabled.");
}
```

You can filter these location update messages based on a distance filter. Changes in position of less than this amount will not generate an update message to the delegate.

```
locationManager.distanceFilter = 1000;  // 1km
```

You can also set a desired level of accuracy; this will determine the location method(s) used by the Core Location framework to determine the user's location.

```
locationManager.desiredAccuracy = kCLLocationAccuracyKilometer;
```

The CLLocationManagerDelegate protocol offers two methods; the first is called when a location update occurs:

```
- (void)locationManager:(CLLocationManager *)manager
        didUpdateToLocation:(CLLocation *)newLocation
        fromLocation:(CLLocation *)oldLocation {
    NSLog(@"Moved from %@ to %@", oldLocation, newLocation);
}
```

The second is called when an error occurs:

```
- (void)locationManager:(CLLocationManager *)manager
        didFailWithError:(NSError *)error {
    NSLog(@"Received Core Location error %@", error);
    [manager stopUpdatingLocation];
}
```

If the location manager is not able to ascertain the user's location immediately, it reports a kCLErrorLocationUnknown error and keeps trying. In most cases you can choose to ignore the error and wait for a new event. However, if the user denies your application access to the location service, the manager will report a kCLErrorDenied error. Upon receiving such an error, you should stop the location manager, as shown in the last snippet.

Reporting the User's Position

Let's build a simple application that reports the user's position and course, and the accuracy to which the device knows this information.

Open Xcode, choose Create a new Xcode project in the startup window, and then choose the Single View Application template from the iOS section of the New Project popup window. When prompted, name your new project **Location**. In the Company Identifier box, enter the root part of your Bundle Identifier (see the iOS Provisioning Portal) used in your Provisioning Profile; for me, this is *uk.co.babilim*. You should leave the Class Prefix box blank, and ensure that the Device Family is set to iPhone, the checkbox for ARC is ticked, and the boxes for storyboard and unit tests are not ticked.

Save your project, and when the Xcode project window opens, add the Core Location framework.

Click the project icon at the top of the Project pane in Xcode, click the main Target for the project, and then click the Build Phases tab. Finally, click the Link Binary with Libraries item to open up the list of linked frameworks, and click the + symbol to add a new framework. Select the Core Location framework (*CoreLocation.framework*) from the drop-down list and click the Add button to add the framework to your project.

Now click the Supporting Files group in Project navigator, and then click the *Location_Prefix.pch* file to open it in the standard editor. Instead of having to include the framework every time you need it, you can use the this header file to import it into all the source files in the project as highlighted in bold below:

```
#ifdef __OBJC__
    #import <Foundation/Foundation.h>
    #import  <UIKit/UIKit.h>
    #import  <CoreLocation/CoreLocation.h>
#endif
```

This file is prefixed to all of your source files. However, the compiler precompiles it separately; this means it does not have to reparse the file on each compile run, which can dramatically speed up your compile times on larger projects.

Now that you've imported the Core Location framework, click the *AppDelegate.h* interface file to open it in the Xcode editor. You're going to use the application delegate to manage the CLLocationManager, so the first thing you need to do at this point is to declare the class as implementing the CLLocationManagerDelegate protocol, declare an instance of the CLLocationManager object in the class declaration, and declare it as a class property.

```
#import <UIKit/UIKit.h>

@class ViewController;

@interface AppDelegate : UIResponder <UIApplicationDelegate,
                                      CLLocationManagerDelegate>

@property (strong, nonatomic) UIWindow *window;
@property (strong, nonatomic) ViewController *viewController;
@property (strong, nonatomic) CLLocationManager *locationManager;

@end
```

Save your changes (⌘-S) and click the corresponding *AppDelegate.m* implementation
file to open it in the Xcode editor. You need to synthesize your `locationManager` property, create an instance of `CLLocationManager`, and start updating your location.

```
#import "AppDelegate.h"
#import "ViewController.h"

@implementation AppDelegate

@synthesize window = _window;
@synthesize viewController = _viewController;
@synthesize locationManager = _locationManager;

- (BOOL)application:(UIApplication *)application
        didFinishLaunchingWithOptions:(NSDictionary *)launchOptions {
    self.window = [[UIWindow alloc] initWithFrame:[[UIScreen mainScreen] bounds]];

    if ( [CLLocationManager locationServicesEnabled] ) {
        self.locationManager = [[CLLocationManager alloc] init];
        self.locationManager.delegate = self;❶
        self.locationManager.distanceFilter = 1000;
        [self.locationManager startUpdatingLocation];
    }

    self.viewController =
        [[ViewController alloc] initWithNibName:@"ViewController" bundle:nil];
    self.window.rootViewController = self.viewController;
    [self.window makeKeyAndVisible];
    return YES;
}

- (void)applicationWillResignActive:(UIApplication *)application {

}

- (void)applicationDidEnterBackground:(UIApplication *)application {

}

- (void)applicationWillEnterForeground:(UIApplication *)application {

}
```

```
- (void)applicationDidBecomeActive:(UIApplication *)application {

}
- (void)applicationWillTerminate:(UIApplication *)application {

}
@end
```

❶ Here, you're specifying that the CLLocationManagerDelegate class is this class, and that delegate methods will be handled by the LocationAppDelegate.

Finally, you need to implement the locationManager:didUpdateToLocation:fromLoca tion: and locationManager:didFailWithError: delegate methods. Add the following two methods to the LocationAppDelegate.m file:

```
- (void)locationManager:(CLLocationManager *)manager
  didUpdateToLocation:(CLLocation *)newLocation
  fromLocation:(CLLocation *)oldLocation {
      NSLog(@"Location: %@", [newLocation description]);
}

- (void)locationManager:(CLLocationManager *)manager
  didFailWithError:(NSError *)error {
      NSLog(@"Error: %@", [error description]);
}
```

At this point, click the Run button in the Xcode tool bar to build and deploy your application into the iPhone Simulator. Since we have yet to build a user interface for the application, you will be presented with a blank gray screen in the Simulator. You'll initially be asked whether you wish to share your location (see Figure 2-1), so click OK to authorize your application.

If you open the Debug area at this point by clicking the middle button of the View segmented control in the Xcode toolbar, you should see something that looks a lot like Figure 2-2.

Figure 2-1. Authorizing Core Location to share your location with your application

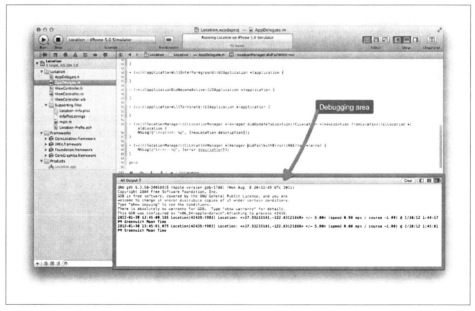

Figure 2-2. The Debugger Console showing the location data returned by the Core Location framework

The two calls to the `locationManager:didUpdateToLocation:fromLocation:` delegate method shown in Figure 2-2 represent an initial fix, and then an update to that initial position. Since I've set the Simulator's position to correspond to Apple's headquarters at 1 Infinite Loop, Cupertino, CA 95014, Simulator's position was reported as latitude 37.3323 North and longitude 122.0307 West.

In the past, the iPhone Simulator reported its location as being at Lat. +37° 19′ 57.74 Long. −122° 1′ 50.39″, corresponding to 1 Infinite Loop, Cupertino, CA. With the arrival of Xcode 4.2, the Simulator can now report your actual position (based on the WiFi position of your development machine).

Alternatively, you can use the Debug→Location menu item in the iOS Simulator to choose to use a different custom location or to choose a simulated run, bike ride, or freeway car journey.

Adding a User Interface

Now extend your code to present the location in a slightly more user-friendly format. You're going to use a `UITableView` to present the information to the user. Click the *ViewController.h* interface file to open it in the Standard editor. You're going to declare that the class handles the `UITableViewDelegate` and `UITableViewDataSource` protocols, so declare a `UITableView` object, and mark it as an `IBOutlet` and a class property:

```
#import <UIKit/UIKit.h>

@interface ViewController : UIViewController
                <UITableViewDelegate, UITableViewDataSource>

@property (strong, nonatomic) IBOutlet UITableView *tableView;

@end
```

Save your changes, click the corresponding *LocationViewController.m* implementation file, and open it in the Xcode editor. Here, you're first going to synthesize the `table View` property and implement the minimum `UITableViewDelegate` and `UITableViewData Source` methods needed:

```
#import "ViewController.h"

@implementation ViewController

@synthesize tableView = _tableView;

- (void)didReceiveMemoryWarning {
    [super didReceiveMemoryWarning];
}

#pragma mark - View lifecycle
```

```
- (void)viewDidLoad {
    [super viewDidLoad];
}

- (void)viewDidUnload {
    [super viewDidUnload];
}

- (void)viewWillAppear:(BOOL)animated {
    [super viewWillAppear:animated];
}

- (void)viewDidAppear:(BOOL)animated {
    [super viewDidAppear:animated];
}

- (void)viewWillDisappear:(BOOL)animated {
    [super viewWillDisappear:animated];
}

- (void)viewDidDisappear:(BOOL)animated {
    [super viewDidDisappear:animated];
}

- (BOOL)shouldAutorotateToInterfaceOrientation:
        (UIInterfaceOrientation)interfaceOrientation {
    return (interfaceOrientation != UIInterfaceOrientationPortraitUpsideDown);
}

#pragma mark UITableViewDelegate Methods

- (void)tableView:(UITableView *)tv
        didSelectRowAtIndexPath:(NSIndexPath *)indexPath {
    // Add code here
}

#pragma mark UITableViewDataSource Methods

- (NSInteger)numberOfSectionsInTableView:(UITableView *)tv {
    return 1;
}

- (NSInteger) tableView:(UITableView *)tv numberOfRowsInSection:(NSInteger) section {
    return 5;
}

- (UITableViewCell *)tableView:(UITableView *)tv
        cellForRowAtIndexPath:(NSIndexPath *)indexPath  {

    static NSString *identifier = @"cell";
    UITableViewCell *cell =
    [tv dequeueReusableCellWithIdentifier:@"cell"];
    if ( cell == nil ) {
        cell = [[UITableViewCell alloc] initWithStyle:UITableViewCellStyleDefault
                                      reuseIdentifier:identifier];
```

```
            cell.accessoryType = UITableViewCellAccessoryNone;
        }
        return cell;

    }

    @end
```

Now click the *ViewController.xib* to open the nib file in Interface Builder.

Drag and drop a `UITableView` from the Object Library into the View, then in the Attributes inspector tab of the Utilities panel change the Table View Style to "Grouped" using the drop-down menu, as shown in Figure 2-3.

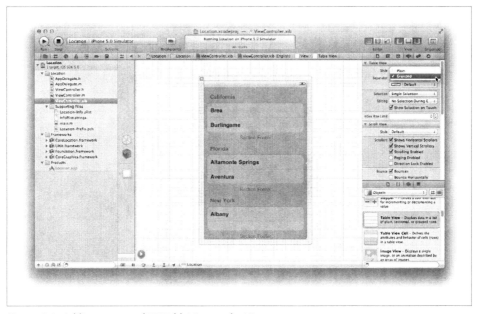

Figure 2-3. Adding a grouped UITableView to the View

Right-click and drag from the File's Owner icon in the dock (the yellow wireframe at the top of the dock) to the Table View to connect the `tableView` outlet in your code to the Table View in the nib, then right-click and drag from the Table View to the File's Owner icon to connect the `dataSource` and `delegate` outlets, as shown in Figure 2-4.

Make sure you've saved your changes to the nib file (⌘-S) and click the Run button on the Xcode toolbar. After the application has been built and deployed into the iPhone Simulator, if everything goes well you should see something very much like Figure 2-5. You should also still see the Simulator's position reported in the Debug area, as in Figure 2-1.

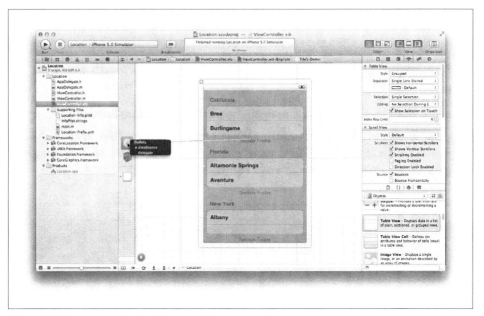

Figure 2-4. Connecting the dataSource and delegate outlets

Figure 2-5. The grouped UITableView

You're almost there. You now need to connect your location manager object and your user interface. You're going to implement this by storing the position values in an NSMutableArray inside the application delegate. You'll use this array to populate UITableViewCell, updating the values stored in this array on each locationMan ager:didUpdateToLocation:fromLocation: message, afterwards instructing your UITableView to reload its data to update your user interface.

Click the *AppDelegate.h* interface file to open it in the Xcode editor and add a NSMutable Array property.

```
#import <UIKit/UIKit.h>

@class ViewController;

@interface AppDelegate : UIResponder <UIApplicationDelegate,CLLocationManagerDelegate>

@property (strong, nonatomic) UIWindow *window;
@property (strong, nonatomic) ViewController *viewController;
@property (strong, nonatomic) CLLocationManager *locationManager;
@property (strong, nonatomic) NSMutableArray *rows;

@end
```

Then, in the corresponding *AppDelegate.m* implementation file, you need to @synthe size the rows property,

```
@synthesize rows = _rows;
```

before initializing it inside the application:didFinishLaunchingWithOptions: method:

```
self.rows = [[NSMutableArray alloc] initWithCapacity:5];
[self.rows insertObject:@"Lat." atIndex:0];
[self.rows insertObject:@"Long." atIndex:1];
[self.rows insertObject:@"Alt." atIndex:2];
[self.rows insertObject:@"Speed" atIndex:3];
[self.rows insertObject:@"Course" atIndex:4];
```

You then need to add code to the locationManager:didUpdateToLocation:fromLoca tion: method to update the rows array and refresh the view controller's tableView property:

```
NSString *latitude = [NSString stringWithFormat:@"Lat. %f degrees",
                        newLocation.coordinate.latitude];
NSString *longitude = [NSString stringWithFormat:@"Long. %f degrees",
                        newLocation.coordinate.longitude];
NSString *altitude =
    [NSString stringWithFormat:@"Alt. %f m", newLocation.altitude];
NSString *speed = [NSString stringWithFormat:@"Speed %f m/s", newLocation.speed];
NSString *course =
    [NSString stringWithFormat:@"Course %f degrees", newLocation.course];

[self.rows insertObject:latitude atIndex:0];
[self.rows insertObject:longitude atIndex:1];
[self.rows insertObject:altitude atIndex:2];
[self.rows insertObject:speed atIndex:3];
```

```
    [self.rows insertObject:course atIndex:4];

    [self.viewController.tableView reloadData];
```

Afterwards, click on the *ViewController.m* implementation file and import the *App-Delegate.h* interface file:

```
#import "AppDelegate.h"
```

Then, modify the `tableView:cellForRowAtIndexPath:` method:

```
- (UITableViewCell *)tableView:(UITableView *)tv
      cellForRowAtIndexPath:(NSIndexPath *)indexPath  {

    static NSString *identifier = @"cell";
    UITableViewCell *cell =
    [tv dequeueReusableCellWithIdentifier:@"cell"];
    if ( cell == nil ) {
        cell = [[UITableViewCell alloc] initWithStyle:UITableViewCellStyleDefault
                                reuseIdentifier:identifier];
        cell.accessoryType = UITableViewCellAccessoryNone;
    }
    AppDelegate *delegate =
        (AppDelegate *)[[UIApplication sharedApplication] delegate];
    cell.textLabel.text = [delegate.rows objectAtIndex:indexPath.row];

    return cell;
}
```

Now you're done. Save your changes and click the Run button to build and deploy the application into the iPhone Simulator. When the application starts up you should see something that resembles Figure 2-6.

Significant Location Monitoring

Along with a Standard Location service, iOS also offers a Significant Location Monitoring service that relies on the availability of cellular radio hardware on your iOS device as it functions using cell-positioning. This offers large power savings and the ability to receive location updates, even if your application is not running and has been backgrounded.

> The Significant Location Monitoring service is available on devices running iOS 4.0 or later, that have a cellular radio (iPhone and iPad with 3G only).

Enabling significant location change service is almost identical to the standard location service, instead of calling the `startUpdatingLocation` method:

```
[locationManager startUpdatingLocation];
```

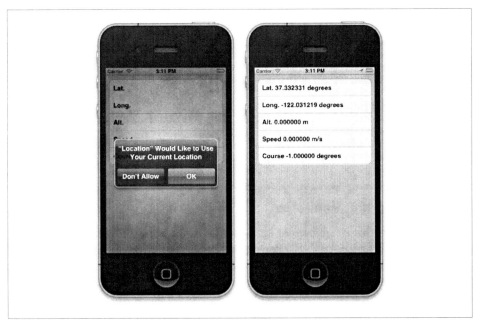

Figure 2-6. The Location application asking for permission to use your location (left), and the populated table view (right)

Instead, you call `startMonitoringSignificantLocationChanges`:

```
[locationManager startMonitoringSignificantLocationChanges];
```

Event messages are sent to `locationManager:didUpdateToLocation:fromLocation:` and `locationManager:didFailWithError:` delegate methods as before.

Open the *Location* project in Xcode, click the *AppDelegate.h* interface file to open it in the standard editor, and modify the `application:didFinishLaunchingWithOptions:` method to use Significant Location Monitoring rather than Standard Location Monitoring, as highlighted below:

```
- (BOOL)application:(UIApplication *)application
       didFinishLaunchingWithOptions:(NSDictionary *)launchOptions {
    self.window = [[UIWindow alloc] initWithFrame:[[UIScreen mainScreen] bounds]];

    if ( [CLLocationManager locationServicesEnabled] ) {
        self.locationManager = [[CLLocationManager alloc] init];
        self.locationManager.delegate = self;
        if ( [CLLocationManager significantLocationChangeMonitoringAvailable] ) {
            [self.locationManager startMonitoringSignificantLocationChanges];
        } else {
            NSLog(@"Significant location change service not available.");
        }
    } else {
        NSLog(@"Location services not enabled.");
    }
```

```
    self.rows = [[NSMutableArray alloc] initWithCapacity:5];
    [self.rows insertObject:@"Lat." atIndex:0];
    [self.rows insertObject:@"Long." atIndex:1];
    [self.rows insertObject:@"Alt." atIndex:2];
    [self.rows insertObject:@"Speed" atIndex:3];
    [self.rows insertObject:@"Course" atIndex:4];

    self.viewController =
        [[ViewController alloc] initWithNibName:@"ViewController" bundle:nil];
    self.window.rootViewController = self.viewController;
    [self.window makeKeyAndVisible];
    return YES;
}
```

Continuous Location Monitoring

Most applications that make use of Significant Location Monitoring need to be aware of the location of the device at all times. Inherent in the design of the Significant Location service is that the event messages it dispatches to its delegate are few and far between. Your application probably won't be running in the foreground to receive these event messages.

To make use of Significant Location Monitoring, it's necessary for your application to have the ability to be backgrounded and handle location event messages in the background while other applications are running in the foreground.

 Because resources are more limited on iOS devices, the operating system limits what your application can do to improve battery life and to improve the user's experience with currently running foreground applications.

Most applications that would make use of Significant Location Monitoring will need to be capable of Continuous Location Monitoring. To notify the operating system that you require this access, you need to add a background mode to your application's *Info.plist* file.

Open your project's *Info.plist* file in the Xcode standard editor and right-click on the last row of the list and select Add Row. In the drop-down menu, select (or type) **Required background modes** and hit Return (see Figure 2-7).

Click the arrow to the left of the key to expand the array and select App registers for location updates (see Figure 2-8).

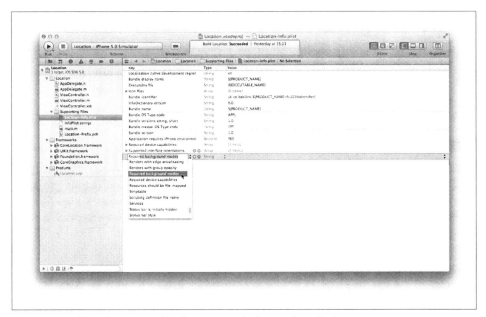

Figure 2-7. Adding the Required background modes key to the Info.plist

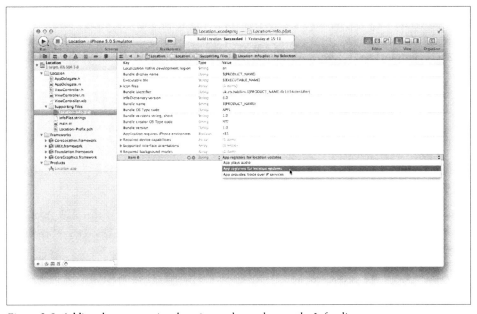

Figure 2-8. Adding the app requires location update values to the Info.plist

Once this key is set, if your application is put into the background, then location event notifications will be delivered to your application.

If you enable your application for Continuous Location Monitoring in the background and turn on the Standard Location service rather than the Significant Location Monitoring service, then while you will receive accurate regular positioning in the background, your application will drain your user's battery very quickly in just a few hours. Don't do this unless you're writing an application that needs continuous accurate positioning, such as a turn-by-turn navigation application.

Sending Your Location to a Database

Since your application is going to be running in the background most of the time, you need to do something other than display your location updates; you're going to have to save the location updates as they arrive into your code so when the user reopens your application at a later time, they have access to them. The easiest way to do this is by using a database.

Adding a database to your project

Let's create a database for the Location application. Take a look at the `locationMan ager:didUpdateToLocation:fromLocation:` delegate callback inside the main application delegate class. The `newLocation` object passed to the delegate contains a time stamp, a latitude and longitude, and altitude measurements as well as values for speed, course, and a measure of the accuracy of the horizontal (latitude and longitude) and vertical (altitude) measurements. You need to put all this information into a database table. For this example, use SQLite, an embeddable SQL engine that comes with the iOS SDK.

If you don't want to create the database for the City Guide application yourself, you can download a prebuilt copy containing the starter cities from this book's website (*http://programmingiphonesensors.com/*).

Open a Terminal window, and at the command prompt type the code shown in bold:

```
$ sqlite3 location.db
```

This will create a database and start SQLite in interactive mode. At the SQL prompt, you need to create your database tables to store your information. Type the code shown in bold (`sqlite>` and `...>` are the SQLite command prompts):

```
SQLite version 3.7.1
Enter ".help" for instructions
Enter SQL statements terminated with a ";"
sqlite> CREATE TABLE location (id INTEGER PRIMARY KEY AUTOINCREMENT,
   ...> timestamp TEXT, latitude REAL, longitude REAL, altitude REAL,
   ...> horizontalAccuracy REAL, verticalAccuracy REAL, speed REAL,
   ...> course REAL);
sqlite> .quit
```

At this stage, you have an empty database and associated table (see Figure 2-9).

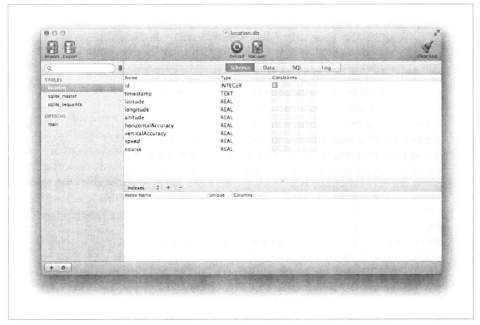

Figure 2-9. Inspecting the location.db file in the Menial Software's Base 2 application

The public domain SQLite library (*http://www.sqlite.org*) is a lightweight transactional database. The library is included in the iOS SDK and will probably do most of the heavy lifting you need for your application to store data. The SQLite engine powers several large applications on Mac OS X, including the Apple Mail application, and is extensively used by the latest generation of browsers to support HTML5 database features. Despite the "Lite" name, the library should not be underestimated.

Interestingly, unlike most SQL database engines, the SQLite engine makes use of dynamic typing. Most other SQL databases implement static typing: the column in which a value is stored determines the type of value. Using SQLite, the column type specifies only the type affinity (the recommended type) for the data stored in that column. However, any column may still store data of any type.

You're now going to add the location database to your application. Open the Finder again and navigate to the directory where you created the *location.db* database file. Open the *Location* project in Xcode, then drag and drop it into the Supporting Files folder of the *Location* project in Xcode. Remember to check the box to indicate that Xcode should "Copy items into destination group's folder."

It's easy enough to create our database from the command line; however, if you're going to be spending a lot of time dealing with databases, you might want to invest in a good graphical application to inspect and manipulate them. I generally use Menial Software's *Base 2* application (*http://menial.co.uk/software/base/*).

To access your database from your code, you'll be using the SQLite library, so you'll need to add it to your project. Click the project icon in the Project Navigator panel in Xcode and go to the Build Phases tab of the Project Info window. Click the Link Binaries with Libraries and click + to add the `libsqlite3.dylib` library. Now, click the Build Settings tab and then click the All button in the tool ribbon to show all of the settings (if it's not already checked). Go to the Search Paths subsection in this window, and in the Linking subsection of this window, double-click on the Other Linker Flags field and click +. Add `-lsqlite3` to the flags and then click OK.

Dealing with the database

Although you've copied the database into your project bundle, you don't want to modify that database *in situ*. Instead, the first time the user opens your application, you'll copy your empty "template" database into the application's Documents directory. This has several advantages: you can safely modify it there without disturbing your original copy of the database, and your database along with your user's data will be automatically backed up when they back up their phone, either to iTunes or into the Cloud.

Click the *AppDelegate.h* interface file to open it in the Xcode editor and add the two method declarations highlighted below:

```
#import <UIKit/UIKit.h>

@class ViewController;

@interface AppDelegate : UIResponder <UIApplicationDelegate,
    CLLocationManagerDelegate>

@property (strong, nonatomic) UIWindow *window;
@property (strong, nonatomic) ViewController *viewController;
@property (strong, nonatomic) CLLocationManager *locationManager;
@property (strong, nonatomic) NSMutableArray *rows;

- (NSString *)databaseLocation;
- (void)copyDatabaseFromBundle;

@end
```

Then in the corresponding *AppDelegate.m* implementation file, add the corresponding method implementations:

```
- (NSString *)databaseLocation {
    NSArray *paths = NSSearchPathForDirectoriesInDomains(NSDocumentDirectory,
```

```
            NSUserDomainMask, YES);
    NSString *documentsPath = [paths objectAtIndex:0];
    NSString *filePath=[documentsPath stringByAppendingPathComponent:@"location.db"];
    return filePath;
}

- (void)copyDatabaseFromBundle {
    NSFileManager *fileManager = [NSFileManager defaultManager];
    NSString *filePath = [self databaseLocation];

    // We don't have a database, maybe this is the first time we've been run?
    if ( ![fileManager fileExistsAtPath:filePath] ) {
        NSString *bundlePath = [[[NSBundle mainBundle] resourcePath]
            stringByAppendingPathComponent:@"location.db"];
        [fileManager copyItemAtPath:bundlePath toPath:filePath error:nil];
    }
}
```

You now need to modify your `application:didFinishLaunchingWithOptions:` method to copy the database from your bundle into the Documents directory when the application starts.

```
- (BOOL)application:(UIApplication *)application
        didFinishLaunchingWithOptions:(NSDictionary *)launchOptions {
    self.window = [[UIWindow alloc] initWithFrame:[[UIScreen mainScreen] bounds]];

    // Copy the starter location database to the Documents directory if needed
    [self copyDatabaseFromBundle];

    if ( [CLLocationManager locationServicesEnabled] ) {
        self.locationManager = [[CLLocationManager alloc] init];
        self.locationManager.delegate = self;
        self.locationManager.distanceFilter = 1000;
        [self.locationManager startUpdatingLocation];
    }
    self.rows = [[NSMutableArray alloc] initWithCapacity:5];
    [self.rows insertObject:@"Lat." atIndex:0];
    [self.rows insertObject:@"Long." atIndex:1];
    [self.rows insertObject:@"Alt." atIndex:2];
    [self.rows insertObject:@"Speed" atIndex:3];
    [self.rows insertObject:@"Course" atIndex:4];

    self.viewController =
        [[ViewController alloc] initWithNibName:@"ViewController" bundle:nil];
    self.window.rootViewController = self.viewController;
    [self.window makeKeyAndVisible];
    return YES;
}
```

Now add two convenience routines, which allow you to read and write locations to the database. Click the *AppDelegate.h* interface file to open it in the Xcode editor and add two more method declarations below the ones you added earlier:

```
- (CLLocation *)readLocationFromDatabaseWithIndex:(int)index;
- (void)addLocationToDatabase:(CLLocation *)newLocation;
```

In the corresponding *AppDelegate.m* implementation file, include the `sqlite3.h` header file,

```
#include <sqlite3.h>
```

before adding the implementations of the two new methods:

```objc
-(void) addLocationToDatabase:(CLLocation *)newLocation {

    sqlite3 *database;

    if(sqlite3_open([[self databaseLocation] UTF8String], &database) == SQLITE_OK) {
        const char *sqlStatement = "INSERT INTO location (timestamp, latitude, "
                                   " longitude, altitude, horizontalAccuracy, "
                                   " verticalAccuracy, speed, course) "
                                   "VALUES (?, ?, ?, ?, ?, ?, ?, ?)";
        sqlite3_stmt *compiledStatement;
        if(sqlite3_prepare_v2(database, sqlStatement, -1,
                &compiledStatement, NULL) == SQLITE_OK)     {

            sqlite3_bind_text(compiledStatement, 1,
                [[newLocation.timestamp description] UTF8String], -1, SQLITE_TRANSIENT);
            sqlite3_bind_double(compiledStatement, 2, newLocation.coordinate.latitude);
            sqlite3_bind_double(compiledStatement, 3, newLocation.coordinate.longitude);
            sqlite3_bind_double(compiledStatement, 4, newLocation.altitude);
            sqlite3_bind_double(compiledStatement, 5, newLocation.horizontalAccuracy);
            sqlite3_bind_double(compiledStatement, 6, newLocation.verticalAccuracy);
            sqlite3_bind_double(compiledStatement, 7, newLocation.speed);
            sqlite3_bind_double(compiledStatement, 8, newLocation.course);

        }
        if(sqlite3_step(compiledStatement) != SQLITE_DONE ) {
            NSLog( @"Error: %s", sqlite3_errmsg(database) );
        } else {
            NSLog( @"Insert into row id = %d",
                (int)sqlite3_last_insert_rowid(database));
        }
        sqlite3_finalize(compiledStatement);
    }
    sqlite3_close(database);

}


- (CLLocation *)readLocationFromDatabaseWithIndex:(int)index {

    CLLocation *location = nil;
    sqlite3 *database;

    if(sqlite3_open([[self databaseLocation] UTF8String], &database) == SQLITE_OK) {
        const char *sqlStatement = [[NSString stringWithFormat:
            @"SELECT * FROM location WHERE id = '%d'", index]
            cStringUsingEncoding:NSASCIIStringEncoding];
        sqlite3_stmt *compiledStatement;
        if(sqlite3_prepare_v2(database, sqlStatement,
                            -1, &compiledStatement, NULL) == SQLITE_OK) {
            if(sqlite3_step(compiledStatement) == SQLITE_ROW) {
```

```
            NSString *timestamp = [NSString stringWithUTF8String:(char *)
                sqlite3_column_text(compiledStatement, 1)];

            // Convert string to date object
            NSDateFormatter *dateFormat = [[NSDateFormatter alloc] init];
            [dateFormat setDateFormat:@"%Y-%m-%d %H:%M:%S %z"];
            NSDate *date = [dateFormat dateFromString:timestamp];

            float latitude = sqlite3_column_double(compiledStatement, 2);
            float longitude = sqlite3_column_double(compiledStatement, 3);
            float altitude = sqlite3_column_double(compiledStatement, 4);
            float horizontalAccuracy= sqlite3_column_double(compiledStatement, 5);
            float verticalAccuracy = sqlite3_column_double(compiledStatement, 6);
            float speed = sqlite3_column_double(compiledStatement, 7);
            float course = sqlite3_column_double(compiledStatement, 8);

            CLLocationCoordinate2D coordinate =
                CLLocationCoordinate2DMake(latitude, longitude);
            location = [[CLLocation alloc]
                initWithCoordinate:coordinate
                altitude:(CLLocationDistance)altitude
                horizontalAccuracy:(CLLocationAccuracy)horizontalAccuracy
                verticalAccuracy:(CLLocationAccuracy)verticalAccuracy
                course:(CLLocationDirection)course
                speed:(CLLocationSpeed)speed timestamp:date];
        }
    }
    sqlite3_finalize(compiledStatement);
    }
    sqlite3_close(database);
    return location;
}
```

Now start serializing your location events to your backend database. In the `location` `Manager:didUpdateToLocation:fromLocation:` method, add a call to your `addLocation` `ToDatabase:` method.

```
- (void)locationManager:(CLLocationManager *)manager
        didUpdateToLocation:(CLLocation *)newLocation
        fromLocation:(CLLocation *)oldLocation {
    NSString *latitude = [NSString stringWithFormat:@"Lat. %f degrees",
                                newLocation.coordinate.latitude];
    NSString *longitude = [NSString stringWithFormat:@"Long. %f degrees",
                                 newLocation.coordinate.longitude];
    NSString *altitude = [NSString stringWithFormat:@"Alt. %f m",
                                newLocation.altitude];
    NSString *speed = [NSString stringWithFormat:@"Speed %f m/s",
                            newLocation.speed];

    NSString *course = [NSString stringWithFormat:@"Course %f degrees",
                             newLocation.course];

    [self.rows insertObject:latitude atIndex:0];
    [self.rows insertObject:longitude atIndex:1];
```

```
[self.rows insertObject:altitude atIndex:2];
[self.rows insertObject:speed atIndex:3];
[self.rows insertObject:course atIndex:4];

[self addLocationToDatabase:newLocation];

[self.viewController.tableView reloadData];
}
```

You've reached a good point to test your code. Save your changes and click the Run button to build and deploy the application onto your device. If all goes well, you should get something that looks identical to what you saw in Figure 2-6. However, if you look in the Debug area, you should see a message generated in the addLocationToData base: method that reports that it successfully inserted the data into the first row of our database, Insert into row id = 0.

Now add an extra row to your table view so that when you open the application you can keep track of how many positions you've recorded into the database. Click the *AppDelegate.h* interface file to open it in the Xcode editor and click one final method declaration below those we added earlier: (int)getSizeOfDatabase;. In the corresponding implementation file, add the method:

```
- (int)getSizeOfDatabase {

    int count = 0;
    sqlite3 *database;

    if (sqlite3_open([[self databaseLocation] UTF8String], &database) == SQLITE_OK)
    {
        const char* sqlStatement = "SELECT COUNT(*) FROM location";
        sqlite3_stmt* statement;

        if (sqlite3_prepare_v2(database, sqlStatement, -1, &statement, NULL) ==
                SQLITE_OK ) {
            if( sqlite3_step(statement) == SQLITE_ROW )
                count = sqlite3_column_int(statement, 0);
        }
        else
        {
            NSLog( @"Failed from sqlite3_prepare_v2. Error is:  %s",
                sqlite3_errmsg(database) );
        }

        // Finalize and close database.
        sqlite3_finalize(statement);
        sqlite3_close(database);
    }

    return count;
}
```

Save your changes, click the *ViewController.m* implementation file, and make the changes highlighted below to the UITableView delegate and data source methods:

```
- (NSInteger)numberOfSectionsInTableView:(UITableView *)tv {
    return 2;
}

- (NSInteger) tableView:(UITableView *)tv numberOfRowsInSection:(NSInteger) section {
    if ( section == 0 ) {
        return 5;
    } else {
        return 1;
    }
}

- (UITableViewCell *)tableView:(UITableView *)tv
        cellForRowAtIndexPath:(NSIndexPath *)indexPath  {

    static NSString *identifier = @"cell";
    UITableViewCell *cell =
    [tv dequeueReusableCellWithIdentifier:@"cell"];
    if ( cell == nil ) {
        cell = [[UITableViewCell alloc] initWithStyle:UITableViewCellStyleDefault
                                  reuseIdentifier:identifier];
        cell.accessoryType = UITableViewCellAccessoryNone;
    }
    AppDelegate *delegate=(AppDelegate *)[[UIApplication sharedApplication] delegate];
    if ( indexPath.section == 0 ) {
        cell.textLabel.text = [delegate.rows objectAtIndex:indexPath.row];
    } else {
        cell.textLabel.text = [NSString stringWithFormat:@"Positions %d",
            [delegate getSizeOfDatabase]];
    }
    return cell;

}
```

Save your changes and click the Run button to build and deploy the application onto your device; you should see something a lot like Figure 2-10.

Bear in mind that the application is using the Significant Location change monitoring API, so locations will only be logged when there is actually a significant change in your location (for instance, if you move between cell towers).

If Standard Location Monitoring is enabled by the foreground application (e.g., a navigation application while driving) while your application is backgrounded and signed up for Significant Location Monitoring, you'll get to take advantage of those much more accurate positions generated by the GPS.

Figure 2-10. The application showing the number of locations logged to the database

Getting the results from your device

You'll need to leave the application running in the background on your device for a few days to see anything interesting going on, and this is also going to give you an idea of the effect that running this sort of service continuously is going to have on the battery life of your device.

However, once you've done that for a few days, the easiest way to take a look at your data is actually to pull it directly from your device using Xcode.

Connect your iPhone to your Mac and open up Xcode, then click Window→Organizer (⇧⌘2) in the Xcode menu to open the Organizer window. Click the arrow to the left of your device to expand the drop-down list and click Applications. Select your Location application from the list of deployed apps, and click the Download button to save the application's data to your Desktop (see Figure 2-11).

This will save the data as a file bundle. Right-click and select Show Package Contents to open the bundle in the Finder and show the contents (see Figure 2-12).

Once the bundle opens in the Finder, click the AppData folder and then again on Documents to reveal the application's *location.db* file with your data inside. You can then use your standard tools to investigate your location data, and in Figure 2-13 you'll see my own data accumulated over the course of a couple of months.

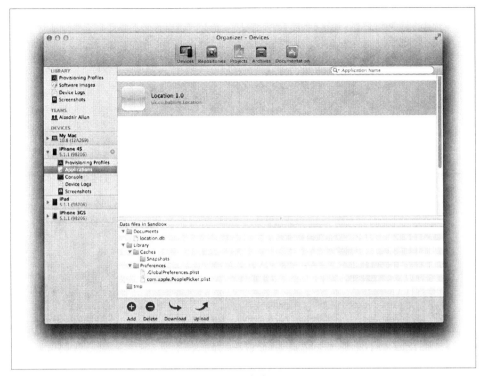

Figure 2-11. Saving the application's data to your desktop

Figure 2-12. Select Show Package Contents to open the bundle in the Finder

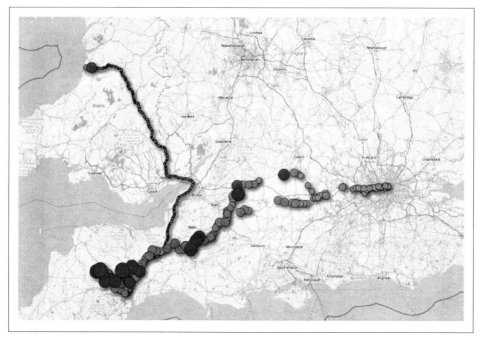

Figure 2-13. My data plotted on a map using openheatmap.com (http://openheatmap.com); the size of the circles represents the horizontal accuracy of the data point

Here I've used a tool to convert the SQLite database file to CSV and then plotted the latitude and longitude values. The size of each data point is the horizontal accuracy of the point using the openheatmap.com (*http://openheatmap.com*) site created by Pete Warden. Larger circles imply that the position isn't well known and comes from cell positioning. Smaller circles imply that the position is from WiFi or GPS positioning.

The bifurcating line heading from my home city of Exeter in the south-west to London in the east shows the two different train routes between the two cities. The large gap in the middle represents when the cell signal has been dropped entirely; there is no cell reception in that region, and no position fixes were obtained by the phone and passed to my code.

Conversely, the trip I took from Exeter up to the Aberystwyth in Wales while the application was running is rather obvious because, during the journey, I had my phone plugged in and running a turn-by-turn navigation application, which was using the standard location service to track my position using the onboard GPS.

These GPS readings were therefore also passed to the Location application running in the background, which is why there is a long trail of very accurate (less than 10 m) position fixes following the M5 motorway and the roads through Wales towards Aberystwyth in the data set.

Region Monitoring

Another capability introduced back in iOS4 is Region Monitoring. Like Significant Location Monitoring, this is based on cell positing and is commonly referred to as *geofencing* since you're effectively setting up a virtual fence around a location. The Region Monitoring service monitors your location and sends events to registered applications when you to cross that "fence."

 At the time of writing, the Region Monitoring service is available only on the iPhone 4, iPhone 4S, and second and third generation 3G iPad running iOS 4.0 or later. While the iPhone 3GS is capable of running iOS 4, it does not have the correct baseband software for Region Monitoring to function. Region Monitoring takes advantage of new functionality in the baseband that arrived with the iPhone 4. Region Monitoring is not available on older models, or on any iOS devices without a cellular radio.

Applications can use Region Monitoring to be notified when the user crosses geographic boundaries. You can use this capability to generate alerts when the user gets close to a specific location.

While you can register more than one region of interest, each region must be registered individually and is given a unique identifier that can be tracked by the application. Each region registered with the operating system can be queried using this unique identifier, and can be updated by your application by registering a new region with the same identifier.

Regions associated with your application are tracked at all times, including when your application is not running. If a region boundary is crossed while an application is not running, that application is relaunched into the background to handle the event. Similarly, if the application is suspended when the event occurs, it is woken up and given a short amount of time to handle the event.

Adding Region Monitoring

Let's add region monitoring to your Location application. Click the *AppDelegate.m* implementation file to open it in the Xcode standard editor and modify the `applica tion:didFinishLaunchingWithOptions:` method, as highlighted below:

```
- (BOOL)application:(UIApplication *)application
        didFinishLaunchingWithOptions:(NSDictionary *)launchOptions {
    self.window = [[UIWindow alloc] initWithFrame:[[UIScreen mainScreen] bounds]];

    [self copyDatabaseFromBundle];

    // Create geo-fence
    CLLocationCoordinate2D center = CLLocationCoordinate2DMake(50.72451, -3.52788);
    CLLocationDistance radius = 200.0; // 200m
```

```
CLRegion *region = [[CLRegion alloc]
    initCircularRegionWithCenter:center
    radius:radius
    identifier:@"Exeter Apple Store"];❶

if ( [CLLocationManager locationServicesEnabled] ) {
    self.locationManager = [[CLLocationManager alloc] init];
    self.locationManager.delegate = self;
    if ( [CLLocationManager significantLocationChangeMonitoringAvailable] ) {
        [self.locationManager startMonitoringSignificantLocationChanges];
    } else {
        NSLog(@"Significant location change service not available.");
    }

    if ( [CLLocationManager regionMonitoringAvailable] ) {
        CLLocationAccuracy accuracy = 1.0;
        [self.locationManager startMonitoringForRegion:region
                                     desiredAccuracy:accuracy];
        NSLog(@"Enabling region monitoring.");
    } else {
        NSLog(@"Warning: Region monitoring not supported on this device.");
    }

} else {
    NSLog(@"Location services not enabled.");
}

self.rows = [[NSMutableArray alloc] initWithCapacity:5];
[self.rows insertObject:@"Lat." atIndex:0];
[self.rows insertObject:@"Long." atIndex:1];
[self.rows insertObject:@"Alt." atIndex:2];
[self.rows insertObject:@"Speed" atIndex:3];
[self.rows insertObject:@"Course" atIndex:4];

self.viewController = [[ViewController alloc]
    initWithNibName:@"ViewController" bundle:nil];
self.window.rootViewController = self.viewController;
[self.window makeKeyAndVisible];

return YES;
}
```

❶ Here, I've set up a geofence of 200 m radius around the Apple Store in the city center of Exeter in the South West of England. You should probably pick a location closer to home.

 If your region is too large, registration of the region fails automatically, so if you are attempting to register a large region, you should check to ensure that this is not larger than the maximum allowed size.

```
if (radius > locationManager.maximumRegionMonitoringDistance) {
    radius = locationManager.maximumRegionMonitoringDistance;
}
```

Next, add the two delegate callbacks:

```
- (void)locationManager:(CLLocationManager *)manager
        didEnterRegion:(CLRegion *)region {

  // stubs method for later
}

- (void)locationManager:(CLLocationManager *)manager
        didExitRegion:(CLRegion *)region {

  // stub method for later
}
```

These are generated, perhaps obviously, when the operating system that detects the device has entered, or exited, from a geofenced region. The region in question, with that unique identifier, will be passed to the delegate method.

> If you have multiple regions, you can tell which one this is by asking the CLRegion object for its identifier:
>
> ```
> NSString *regionName = region.identifier;
> ```

Adding Local Notifications

In most of the common use cases for Region Monitoring, you'll need to notify users when they enter or exit the monitored region. The obvious way to do this is to use Local Notifications, which were introduced in iOS 4. Let's add them to your application so that when the user crosses the boundary of your registered region, he gets a notification on his device.

Click the *AppDelegate.m* implementation file to open it in the Xcode standard editor and modify the application:didFinishLaunchingWithOptions: method as highlighted below:

```
- (BOOL)application:(UIApplication *)application
        didFinishLaunchingWithOptions:(NSDictionary *)launchOptions {
    self.window = [[UIWindow alloc] initWithFrame:[[UIScreen mainScreen] bounds]];

    // Copy the starter location database to the Documents directory if needed
    [self copyDatabaseFromBundle];

    // Create geo-fence
    CLLocationCoordinate2D center = CLLocationCoordinate2DMake(50.72451, -3.52788);
    CLLocationDistance radius = 200.0; // 200m
    CLRegion *region = [[CLRegion alloc] initCircularRegionWithCenter:center
        radius:radius
        identifier:@"Exeter Apple Store"];

    if ( [CLLocationManager locationServicesEnabled] ) {
        self.locationManager = [[CLLocationManager alloc] init];
        self.locationManager.delegate = self;
```

```
        if ( [CLLocationManager significantLocationChangeMonitoringAvailable] ) {
            [self.locationManager startMonitoringSignificantLocationChanges];
        } else {
            NSLog(@"Significant location change service not available.");
        }

        if ( [CLLocationManager regionMonitoringAvailable] ) {
            CLLocationAccuracy accuracy = 1.0;
            [self.locationManager startMonitoringForRegion:region
                desiredAccuracy:accuracy];
            NSLog(@"Enabling region monitoring.");
        } else {
            NSLog(@"Warning: Region monitoring not supported on this device.");
        }

    } else {
        NSLog(@"Location services not enabled.");
    }

    self.rows = [[NSMutableArray alloc] initWithCapacity:5];
    [self.rows insertObject:@"Lat." atIndex:0];
    [self.rows insertObject:@"Long." atIndex:1];
    [self.rows insertObject:@"Alt." atIndex:2];
    [self.rows insertObject:@"Speed" atIndex:3];
    [self.rows insertObject:@"Course" atIndex:4];

    self.viewController = [[ViewController alloc]
        initWithNibName:@"ViewController" bundle:nil];
    self.window.rootViewController = self.viewController;
    [self.window makeKeyAndVisible];

    UILocalNotification *localNotification = [launchOptions
        objectForKey:UIApplicationLaunchOptionsLocalNotificationKey];
    if (localNotification) {
        NSLog(@"Notification Body: %@",localNotification.alertBody);
        NSLog(@"%@", localNotification.userInfo);
    }

    application.applicationIconBadgeNumber = 0;
    [[UIApplication sharedApplication] cancelAllLocalNotifications];

    return YES;
}
```

This will handle the notification if the application is opened due to the arrival of a notification. Similarly in your applicationDidBecomeActive: method, you should provide code to handle the incoming notification if the application is open and being brought into the foreground by the notification.

```
- (void)applicationDidBecomeActive:(UIApplication *)application {
    application.applicationIconBadgeNumber = 0;
    [[UIApplication sharedApplication] cancelAllLocalNotifications];

}
```

Finally, you need to schedule a notification with the operating system from your `loca` `tionManager:didEnterRegion:` and `locationManager:didExitRegion:` methods. Since you want the notification to appear when the user is transiting the boundary of the region, you'll schedule it for the current time (i.e., now).

```
- (void)locationManager:(CLLocationManager *)manager
      didEnterRegion:(CLRegion *)region {

   UILocalNotification *notification = [[UILocalNotification alloc] init];
   notification.fireDate = [NSDate date];
   notification.timeZone = [NSTimeZone defaultTimeZone];

   notification.alertBody = @"Entered Region";
   notification.soundName = UILocalNotificationDefaultSoundName;
   notification.applicationIconBadgeNumber = 1;

   [[UIApplication sharedApplication] scheduleLocalNotification:notification];

}

- (void)locationManager:(CLLocationManager *)manager
      didExitRegion:(CLRegion *)region {

   UILocalNotification *notification = [[UILocalNotification alloc] init];
   notification.fireDate = [NSDate date];
   notification.timeZone = [NSTimeZone defaultTimeZone];

   notification.alertBody = @"Exited Region";
   notification.soundName = UILocalNotificationDefaultSoundName;
   notification.applicationIconBadgeNumber = 1;

   [[UIApplication sharedApplication] scheduleLocalNotification:notification];

}
```

Save your changes and click the Run button in the Xcode toolbar to build and deploy your application onto your device. The easiest way to test this code is to deploy your application onto your device with a suitable geofenced region defined nearby, unplug your device from your Mac, and go for a walk.

If all goes well, as you enter the defined region, you should see something like Figure 2-14.

If your application is open and in the foreground when the notification arrives it will still be placed in the Notification Center by the operating system, but the user will not be given any visual notice that it has occurred. It's up to you to check whether your application is in the foreground and handle the notification appropriately.

Figure 2-14. Notifications as we enter the geofenced region: when the device is locked (left), when it is in use but the application is in the background (middle), and when it is in the iOS Notification Center (right)

CHAPTER 3

Map Kit

The Map Kit framework allows you to embed maps directly into your views, and provides support for annotating these maps and adding overlays. Along with the Core Location framework, it does all the heavy lifting involved in creating and displaying maps in your applications.

Adding a Map

Let's add a map to the Location application you built in the previous chapter. Open up the application in Xcode. The first thing you need to do is add the Map Kit framework to your project. Click the project icon at the top of the Project pane in Xcode, click the main Target for the project, and then click the Build Phases tab. Finally, click the Link Binary with Libraries item to open up the list of linked frameworks, and click the + symbol to add a new framework. Select the *MapKit.framework* from the dropdown list and click the Add button to add the framework to your project.

Now click the Supporting Files group in Project navigator, and then click the *Location_Prefix.pch* file to open it in the standard editor. Instead of having to include the framework every time you need it (as you did in the last chapter), you can use this header file to import it into all the source files in the project, as highlighted in bold below:

```
#ifdef __OBJC__
    #import <Foundation/Foundation.h>
    #import  <UIKit/UIKit.h>
    #import <CoreLocation/CoreLocation.h>
    #import <MapKit/MapKit.h>
#endif
```

Once you've done that, make sure you've saved your changes and click on the *ViewController.xib* file to open it in Interface Builder. Open the Utility panel if it's not already open, then drag and drop a Table View Cell (`UITableViewCell`) from the Object Library into the editor.

Click the Table View Cell to highlight it, and then in the Size Inspector, resize the cell to have W = 300 points (rather than the default cell width of 320 points) and H = 170 points. This will allow the cell to fit easily into the grouped table view mode of our user interface. Next, drag and drop a Map View (`MKMapView`) from the Object Library and position it inside our newly resized table view cell, as shown in Figure 3-1.

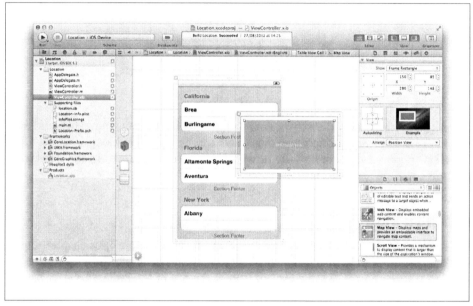

Figure 3-1. Creating the custom UITableViewCell

Save your changes and close the Utility panel, then click to open the Assistant editor. Right-click and drag from the `UITableViewCell` and the `MKMapView` the table view cell contains into the *ViewController.h* interface file to create two more properties called `mapCell` and `mapView` as an `IBOutlet` (see Figure 3-2).

Save your changes and return to the Standard editor, then click the *ViewController.h* interface file to open it. You should see something a lot like this:

```
#import <UIKit/UIKit.h>

@interface ViewController :
    UIViewController <UITableViewDelegate, UITableViewDataSource>

@property (strong, nonatomic) IBOutlet UITableView *tableView;
@property (strong, nonatomic) IBOutlet UITableViewCell *mapCell;
@property (weak, nonatomic) IBOutlet MKMapView *mapView;

@end
```

Now click the corresponding implementation file, *ViewController.m*, to open it in the editor. Here you're going to add a new `UITableViewDataSource` method:

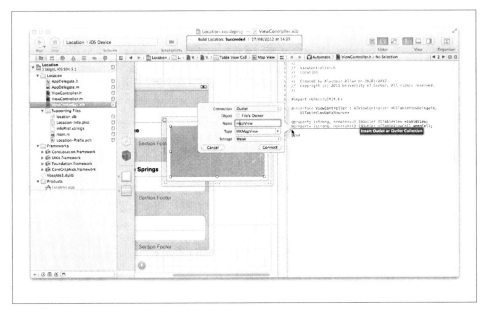

Figure 3-2. Creating the mapCell and mapView properties

```
- (CGFloat)tableView:(UITableView *)tableView
  heightForRowAtIndexPath:(NSIndexPath *)indexPath
{
    NSInteger height;
    if ( indexPath.section == 0 ) {
        height = 170;
    } else {
        height = 44;
    }
    return height;
}
```

Then, modify both the numberOfSectionsInTableView: and the tableView:numberOfRows
InSection: delegate methods.

```
- (NSInteger)numberOfSectionsInTableView:(UITableView *)tv {
    return 3;
}

- (NSInteger) tableView:(UITableView *)tv
       numberOfRowsInSection:(NSInteger) section {
    if ( section == 0 ) {
        return 1;
    } else if ( section == 1 ) {
        return 5;
    } else {
        return 1;
    }
}
```

Here you've added another section to the grouped table view. The first section has only one cell of height H = 170 pixels, and the second section has five rows of height H = 44 pixels, which is the default height for an iPhone `UITableViewCell`. The final section has just one cell with the default height. Now you need to modify `TableView:cellFor RowAtIndexPath:` so that you return your customized map cell in the first section, your location table view cells in the second section, and the number of points in your location database file in the final section.

```
- (UITableViewCell *)tableView:(UITableView *)tv
        cellForRowAtIndexPath:(NSIndexPath *)indexPath  {

    UITableViewCell *cell = nil;
    if ( indexPath.section == 0 ) {
        cell = self.mapCell;

    } else {
        static NSString *identifier = @"cell";
        cell = [tv dequeueReusableCellWithIdentifier:@"cell"];
        if ( cell == nil ) {
            cell = [[UITableViewCell alloc]
                initWithStyle:UITableViewCellStyleDefault
                reuseIdentifier:identifier];
            cell.accessoryType = UITableViewCellAccessoryNone;
        }
        AppDelegate *delegate =
            (AppDelegate *)[[UIApplication sharedApplication] delegate];
        if ( indexPath.section == 1 ) {
            cell.textLabel.text = [delegate.rows objectAtIndex:indexPath.row];
        } else {
            cell.textLabel.text = [NSString stringWithFormat:@"Positions %d",
                [delegate getSizeOfDatabase]];
        }
    }
    return cell;
```

You're almost done, but let's address a subtle user interface issue before deploying your code. If you look at your current interface, the square cornered map inside a round cornered grouped table view cell isn't going to look good. While having an `MKMapView` with curved corners is pretty hard to do inside Interface Builder, you can fix it in code fairly easily.

You're going to use the low level QuartzCore framework to provide the curved corners, so click the project icon at the top of the Project pane in Xcode, click the main Target for the project, and then click the Build Phases tab. Finally, click the Link Binary with Libraries item to open the list of linked frameworks, and click the + symbol to add a new framework. Select the QuartzCore framework (*QuartzCore.framework*) from the drop-down list and click the Add button to add the framework to your project.

Then click the *ViewController.h* interface file to open it in the Xcode editor and import the corresponding header files:

```
#import <QuartzCore/QuartzCore.h>
```

Save your changes, then open the corresponding implementation file, *View-Controller.m*. In the `viewDidLoad:` method add the line in bold below.

```
- (void)viewDidLoad {
    self.mapView.layer.cornerRadius = 10.0;
    [super viewDidLoad];
}
```

You're done. Save your changes and click the Run button in the Xcode toolbar to compile and deploy your application into the iPhone Simulator. If all goes well, you should see something that looks a lot like Figure 3-3.

Figure 3-3. The new user interface

This is okay; however, it's not amazingly exciting. Map Kit knows the user's location and for this to be displayed on the map, you only need to add the following line to the `viewDidLoad:` method:

```
self.mapView.showsUserLocation = YES;
```

Save the change and click the Build and Run button in the Xcode toolbar again. This time you should see something like Figure 3-4.

Figure 3-4. Displaying the user's location on the map

However, while the Map Kit framework is able to mark the user's location on the map, there is no way to monitor it or update the current map view when the location changes. So you're going to implement this functionality using the Core Location framework.

Click on the *AppDelegate.m* implementation file to open it in the editor. Then in the `locationManager:didUpdateLocation:fromLocation:` delegate method, add the lines in bold below:

```
- (void)locationManager:(CLLocationManager *)manager
        didUpdateToLocation:(CLLocation *)newLocation
        fromLocation:(CLLocation *)oldLocation {
    NSLog(@"Location: %@", [newLocation description]);

    NSString *latitude = [NSString stringWithFormat:@"Lat. %f degrees",
                          newLocation.coordinate.latitude];
    NSString *longitude = [NSString stringWithFormat:@"Long. %f degrees",
                          newLocation.coordinate.longitude];
    NSString *altitude = [NSString stringWithFormat:@"Alt. %f m",
        newLocation.altitude];
    NSString *speed = [NSString stringWithFormat:@"Speed %f m/s",
        newLocation.speed];

    NSString *course = [NSString stringWithFormat:@"Course %f degrees",
        newLocation.course];
```

```
[self.rows insertObject:latitude atIndex:0];
[self.rows insertObject:longitude atIndex:1];
[self.rows insertObject:altitude atIndex:2];
[self.rows insertObject:speed atIndex:3];
[self.rows insertObject:course atIndex:4];

[self addLocationToDatabase:newLocation];

[self.viewController.tableView reloadData];

double miles = 2.0;
double scalingFactor =
    ABS( cos(2 * M_PI * newLocation.coordinate.latitude /360.0) );

MKCoordinateSpan span;
span.latitudeDelta = miles/69.0;
span.longitudeDelta = miles/( scalingFactor*69.0 );
MKCoordinateRegion region;
region.span = span;
region.center = newLocation.coordinate;

[self.viewController.mapView setRegion:region animated:YES];

}
```

Here you set the map region to be 2 square miles, centered on the current location, and then zoom in and display the current user location.

 The number of miles spanned by a degree of longitude range varies based on the current latitude. For example, 1 degree of longitude spans a distance of about 69 miles at the equator but shrinks to 0 at the poles. However, unlike longitudinal distances that vary based on the latitude, 1 degree of latitude is always about 69 miles (ignoring variations due to the slightly ellipsoidal shape of the Earth). The length of 1 degree of Longitude (in miles) equals the cosine of the latitude × 69 miles.

Click the Build and Run button on the Xcode toolbar to compile and deploy the application into the iPhone Simulator. Once the application starts, up you should see something much like Figure 3-5.

Figure 3-5. Following the user's location using the Core Location framework

Normally the iPhone will pan and zoom a map when asked to change region, however you'll probably have noticed that this part didn't really work that well. This is because you've wrapped the map inside a table view cell and asked the table view to reload its data inside the same method where you asked the map to `setRegion:animated:`. However, you can make use of the `scheduledTimerWithTimeInterval:target:selector:user Info:repeats:` method to avoid this problem and make your map pan and zoom properly as the table view is updated inside your Core Location delegate method.

To do so, you're going to add a new method `animateMap:`, which you'll call using an `NSTimer` event. The method will contain the code you just added to the Core Location delegate, as below:

```
- (void)locationManager:(CLLocationManager *)manager
    didUpdateToLocation:(CLLocation *)newLocation
           fromLocation:(CLLocation *)oldLocation {
    NSLog(@"Location: %@", [newLocation description]);

    NSString *latitude = [NSString stringWithFormat:@"Lat. %f degrees",
                          newLocation.coordinate.latitude];
    NSString *longitude = [NSString stringWithFormat:@"Long. %f degrees",
                           newLocation.coordinate.longitude];
    NSString *altitude =
        [NSString stringWithFormat:@"Alt. %f m", newLocation.altitude];
```

```
        NSString *speed =
            [NSString stringWithFormat:@"Speed %f m/s", newLocation.speed];

        NSString *course =
            [NSString stringWithFormat:@"Course %f degrees", newLocation.course];

        [self.rows insertObject:latitude atIndex:0];
        [self.rows insertObject:longitude atIndex:1];
        [self.rows insertObject:altitude atIndex:2];
        [self.rows insertObject:speed atIndex:3];
        [self.rows insertObject:course atIndex:4];

        [self addLocationToDatabase:newLocation];

        [self.viewController.tableView reloadData];

        [NSTimer scheduledTimerWithTimeInterval:0.2 target:self
            selector:@selector(animateMap:) userInfo:newLocation repeats:NO];

    }

    - (void)animateMap:(NSTimer *)timer {

        CLLocation *newLocation = (CLLocation *)[timer userInfo];

        double miles = 2.0;
        double scalingFactor =
            ABS( cos(2 * M_PI * newLocation.coordinate.latitude /360.0) );

        MKCoordinateSpan span;
        span.latitudeDelta = miles/69.0;
        span.longitudeDelta = miles/( scalingFactor*69.0 );

        MKCoordinateRegion region;
        region.span = span;
        region.center = newLocation.coordinate;

        [self.viewController.mapView setRegion:region animated:YES];

    }
```

If you save your changes and click the Run button in the Xcode toolbar again, you should see the map panning and zooming as you'd expect as the table view is updated by the Core Location delegate method.

Annotating Maps

Adding simple map annotations using the Map Kit framework is actually pretty easy. The first thing you need to do is create a class that implements the MKAnnotation delegate protocol. Right-click the Location group in the Project Navigator panel and New File to create a new Objective-C class (make it an NSObject subclass). Name the new class SimpleAnnotation when prompted.

Open the *SimpleAnnotation.h* interface file Xcode just created in the Standard editor and modify it as follows:

```
#import <Foundation/Foundation.h>

@interface SimpleAnnotation : NSObject <MKAnnotation>

@property (nonatomic, assign) CLLocationCoordinate2D coordinate;
@property (nonatomic, strong) NSString *title;
@property (nonatomic, strong) NSString *subtitle;

+ (id)annotationWithCoordinate:(CLLocationCoordinate2D)coord;
- (id)initWithCoordinate:(CLLocationCoordinate2D)coord;

@end
```

Then open the corresponding *SimpleAnnotation.m* implementation file and make the changes shown:

```
#import "SimpleAnnotation.h"

@implementation SimpleAnnotation

@synthesize coordinate=_coordinate;
@synthesize title=_title;
@synthesize subtitle=_subtitle;

+ (id)annotationWithCoordinate:(CLLocationCoordinate2D)coord {
  return [[[self class] alloc] initWithCoordinate:coord];
}

- (id)initWithCoordinate:(CLLocationCoordinate2D)coord {
  if ( self = [super init] ) {
    self.coordinate = coord;
  }

  return self;
}

@end
```

The `SimpleAnnotation` class is just a container; it implements the `MKAnnotation` protocol to allow it to hold the coordinates and title (with subtitle) of our annotation.

Click the *ViewController.h* interface file to open in the Xcode editor, and import the `SimpleAnnotation` header file:

```
#import "SimpleAnnotation.h"
```

Then, in the `viewDidLoad:` method, add two annotations to our `mapView` as follows:

```
CLLocationCoordinate2D moffett = {37.4163, -122.0519};
SimpleAnnotation *moffettAnnotation =
  [[SimpleAnnotation alloc] initWithCoordinate:moffett];
moffettAnnotation.title = @"Moffett Federal Airfield";
moffettAnnotation.subtitle = @"37.4163, -122.0519";
```

```
[self.mapView addAnnotation: moffettAnnotation];

CLLocationCoordinate2D sanJose = {37.3647, -121.9338};
SimpleAnnotation *sanJoseAnnotation =
    [[SimpleAnnotation alloc] initWithCoordinate:sanJose];
sanJoseAnnotation.title = @"San Jose International";
sanJoseAnnotation.subtitle = @"37.3647, -121.9338";
[self.mapView addAnnotation: sanJoseAnnotation];
```

Save your changes, and change to the *AppDelagate.m*. You'll have to expand your view a little bit as your map window currently excludes your new markers. Go into the `animateMap:` method and change the size of your view from 2 miles to 20 miles.

```
double miles = 20.0;
```

Then click the Run button in the Xcode toolbar to compile and deploy your application in the iPhone Simulator. If all goes well, you should see something much like Figure 3-6.

Figure 3-6. An annotated map of Cupertino, CA (left) and after tapping on the annotation pin to show the annotation details (right)

Congratulations, you now have an annotated map application that tracks and reports the user's position, and a good grounding with the Core Location and Map Kit frameworks.

Adding Overlays

Adding polygon overlays to your map is almost as easy as adding annotations. So let's go back to your Location application and modify it yet again to add a circular overlay to represent the region you're monitoring. You'll look at other types of overlays, such as image overlays, when you look at heat maps later on in Chapter 6.

So I can easily illustrate what's going on in the iPhone Simulator, I'm going to change the latitude and longitude of my geofenced region (which was previously centered on the Exeter Apple Store) to be centered on San Jose International Airport.

To start with, I'm going to open *AppDelegate.m* in the editor and then in the applica
tion:didFinishLaunchingWithOptions: method I'm going to change the latitude, longitude, and radius of my geofence from:

```
CLLocationCoordinate2D center = CLLocationCoordinate2DMake(50.72451,-3.52788);
CLLocationDistance radius = 200.0; // 200m
```

to:

```
CLLocationCoordinate2D center = CLLocationCoordinate2DMake(37.3647,-121.9338);
CLLocationDistance radius = 3000.0 // 3km
```

These new coordinates define a geographical region centered on San Jose International Airport, which is 3 km (or 1.9 miles) in radius.

 You can keep your own geofenced region as you had it in the last chapter, but remember to change the latitude, longitude, and radius that I'll
use below for the overlay region to be the same as your own geofenced
region.

The first thing you need to do now is to create your overlay. You want to do this in the viewDidAppear: method of your view controller. So click the *ViewController.m* implementation file to open it in the editor and add the following code highlighted below to the method:

```
- (void)viewDidAppear:(BOOL)animated {
    [super viewDidAppear:animated];

    CLLocationCoordinate2D center = CLLocationCoordinate2DMake(37.3647,-121.9338);
    CLLocationDistance radius = 3000.0;
    MKCircle *circle = [MKCircle circleWithCenterCoordinate:center radius:radius];
    [circle setTitle:@" "];
    [self.mapView addOverlay:circle];
}
```

Here, you've defined an MKCircle object and added it to your map view. However, right now your view doesn't really know what to do with this overlay, or how you want it styled. So, you now need to tell it.

Click the *ViewController.h* interface file, and modify it as below to declare your view controller as an `MKMapViewDelegate`:

```
#import <UIKit/UIKit.h>
#import <QuartzCore/QuartzCore.h>

#import "SimpleAnnotation.h"

@interface ViewController : UIViewController <UITableViewDelegate,
    UITableViewDataSource, MKMapViewDelegate>

@property (strong, nonatomic) IBOutlet UITableView *tableView;
@property (strong, nonatomic) IBOutlet UITableViewCell *mapCell;
@property (weak, nonatomic) IBOutlet MKMapView *mapView;

@end
```

Having done so, click the *ViewController.xib* NIB file and right-click and drag from the `MKMapView` inside your `UITableViewCell` to the File's Owner icon at the top of the dock to the left of the editor panel (see Figure 3-7). Connect the view controller to the map view as a delegate.

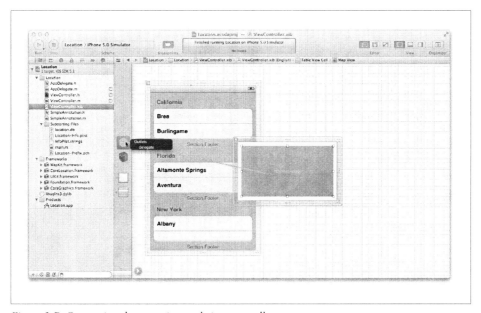

Figure 3-7. Connecting the map view and view controller

Now you need to implement the `mapView:viewForOverlay:` delegate callback:

```
- (MKOverlayView *)mapView:(MKMapView *)mapView
        viewForOverlay:(id <MKOverlay>)overlay {

    NSLog(@"Overlaying circle");
    MKCircle *circle = overlay;
```

```
MKCircleView *circleView = [[MKCircleView alloc] initWithCircle:overlay];

if ([circle.title isEqualToString:@"San Jose Airport"]) {

    circleView.fillColor = [UIColor redColor];
    circleView.alpha = 0.5;
}
return circleView;
}
```

Here, take your `MKCircle` object, which in reality is an `MKOverly` object, and generate a view that the map view can use to plot your overlay on top of its map.

Save your changes and click the Run button to build and deploy into the Simulator. You should see something much like Figure 3-8.

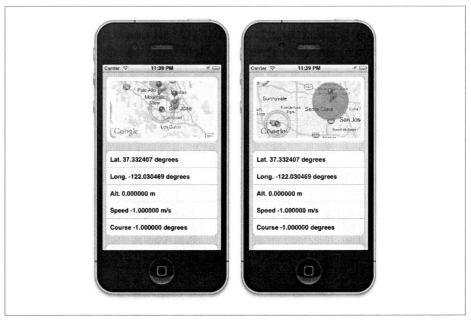

Figure 3-8. The geofenced region is now highlighted with a semi-transparent red circle (left), more clearly seen in the zoomed view (right)

If you're using a geofenced region of your own, based on your current location, now is the time to build and deploy onto your device and go for a walk and test your code out the old fashioned way.

CHAPTER 4

Digital Compass

The digital compass functionality on the iPhone and iPad is provided by a magneto-meter. The magnetometer measures the strength of the magnetic field surrounding the device. However, in the absence of any strong local fields, these measurements will be of the ambient magnetic field of the Earth, allowing the device to determine its "heading" with respect to the geomagnetic North Pole and act as a digital compass. The geomagnetic heading and true heading, relative to the geographical North Pole, can vary widely (by several tens of degrees depending on your location).

About the Magnetometer

The magnetometer will return the heading (or yaw) of the device (see Figure 4-1).

Along with reporting the current location, the CLLocationManager class can report the current heading of the device, in the case where the device's hardware supports it. If location updates are also enabled, the location manager returns both true heading and magnetic heading values. If location updates are not enabled, the location manager returns only the magnetic heading value.

Magnetic heading updates are available even if the user has switched off location updates in the Settings application. Additionally, users are *not* prompted to give permission to use heading data, as it is assumed that magnetic heading information cannot compromise user privacy. On an enabled device, the magnetic heading data should therefore always be available to your application.

As I mentioned previously, the magnetometer readings will be affected by local magnetic fields, so the CLLocationManager may attempt to calibrate its heading readings by displaying a heading calibration panel before it starts to issue update messages (see Figure 4-2).

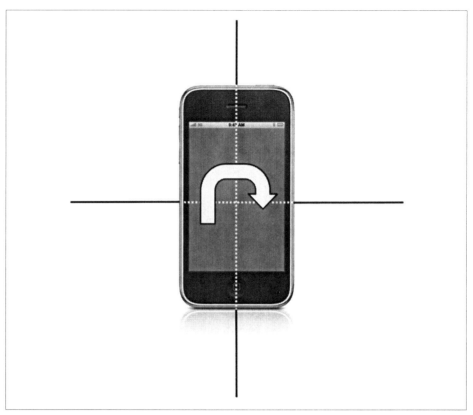

Figure 4-1. Using the magnetometer to determine the heading (yaw) of the device

However, before it does so, it will call the `locationManagerShouldDisplayHeadingCali bration:` delegate method:

```
- (BOOL)locationManagerShouldDisplayHeadingCalibration:
  (CLLocationManager *)manager {
      return YES;
}
```

If you return `YES` from this method, the `CLLocationManager` will display the device calibration panel on top of the current window. The calibration panel prompts the user to move the device in a figure-eight pattern so that Core Location can distinguish between the Earth's magnetic field and any local magnetic fields. The panel will remain visible until calibration is complete or until you dismiss it by calling the `dismissHea dingCalibrationDisplay:` method in the `CLLocationManager` class.

Figure 4-2. The heading calibration panel

Writing a Compass Application

Let's go ahead and implement a simple view-based application to illustrate how to use the magnetometer. Open Xcode and start a new iPhone project, select a View-based Application template, and name the project "Compass" when prompted for a filename.

Since you'll be making use of the Core Location framework, the first thing you need to do is add it to your new project. Click the Compass project file in the Project navigator window on the right in Xcode, select the Target, and click the Build Phases tab. Then, click the Link with Libraries drop-down, and click the + button to open the file popup window. Select *CoreLocation.framework* from the list of available frameworks and click the Add button.

You're going to build an application that will act as a compass, so you're going to need an image of an arrow to act as the compass needle. Download (or draw in the graphics package of your choice) an image of an arrow pointing upwards on a transparent background. Save it as, or convert it to, a PNG format file. Drag and drop this PNG into your Xcode Project; remember to tick the "Copy items into destination group's folder (if needed)" check box in the popup dialog that appears when you drop the files into Xcode.

Click *CompassViewController.xib* to open it in Interface Builder. Drag and drop a UIImageView from the Object Library into the View, positioning it roughly in the center of your window and resizing the bounding box to be a square (as in Figure 4-3). In the Attributes inspector of the Utilities pane set the View mode to be Aspect Fit, uncheck the Opaque checkbox in the Drawing section, and select the arrow image that you added to your project in the Image drop-down.

Next, drag and drop four UILabel elements from the Object Library into the View, position the four labels as in Figure 4-3, and change the text in the left most two to read Magnetic Heading: and True Heading:.

Close the Utility pane and switch from the Standard to the Assistant Editor. Control-click and drag from the two right most UILabel elements to the assistant editor to create a magneticHeadingLabel and trueHeadingLabel outlet, and then again for the UIImageView to create an arrowImage outlet (see Figure 4-3).

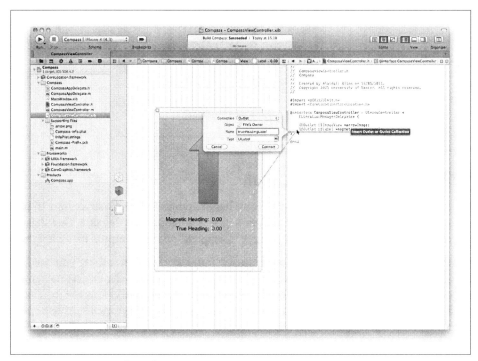

Figure 4-3. Connecting the outlets to the UI elements in Interface Builder

Then click the *CompassViewController.h* interface file and declare the class as a CLLocationManagerDelegate, remembering to import the *CoreLocation.h* header file. After doing so, the interface should look like this:

```
#import <UIKit/UIKit.h>
#import <CoreLocation/CoreLocation.h>
```

```
@interface CompassViewController : UIViewController <CLLocationManagerDelegate> {

    IBOutlet UIImageView *arrowImage;
    IBOutlet UILabel *magneticHeadingLabel;
    IBOutlet UILabel *trueHeadingLabel;
}

@end
```

Save your changes, and click the corresponding *CompassViewController.m* implementation file. Uncomment the `viewDidLoad` method and the following code to the implementation. This will create an instance of the `CLLocationManager` class, and will send both location and heading update messages to the designated delegate class:

```
- (void)viewDidLoad {
    [super viewDidLoad];
    CLLocationManager *locationManager = [[CLLocationManager alloc] init];
    locationManager.delegate = self;
    if( [CLLocationManager locationServicesEnabled]
        && [CLLocationManager headingAvailable]) {❶
        [locationManager startUpdatingLocation];
        [locationManager startUpdatingHeading];
    } else {
        NSLog(@"Can't report heading");
    }
}
```

❶ It is more important to check whether heading information is available than it is to check whether location services are available, as the availability of heading information is restricted to the latest generation of devices.

You can (optionally) filter the heading update messages based on an angular filter. Changes in heading of less than this amount will not generate an update message to the delegate. For example:

```
locationManager.headingFilter = 5;  // 5 degrees
```

The default value of this property is `kCLHeadingFilterNone`. You should use this value if you want to be notified of all heading updates. I'm going to leave the filter set to the default value. However, if you want to filter messages from Core Location this way, add the above line to your `viewDidLoad` method inside the if-block:

```
if( [CLLocationManager locationServicesEnabled]
    && [CLLocationManager headingAvailable]) {
    [locationManager startUpdatingLocation];
    [locationManager startUpdatingHeading];
    locationManager.headingFilter = 5;  // 5 degrees
} else {
    ... code ...
}
```

The `CLLocationManagerDelegate` protocol calls the `locationManager:didUpdateHead ing:` delegate method when the heading is updated. You're going to use this method to update your user interface, so add the following code to your view controller:

```
- (void)locationManager:(CLLocationManager*)manager
        didUpdateHeading:(CLHeading*)newHeading {

    if (newHeading.headingAccuracy > 0) {
        float magneticHeading = newHeading.magneticHeading;
        float trueHeading = newHeading.trueHeading;❶

        magneticHeadingLabel.text = [NSString stringWithFormat:@"%f", magneticHeading];
        trueHeadingLabel.text = [NSString stringWithFormat:@"%f", trueHeading];

        float heading = -1.0f * M_PI * newHeading.magneticHeading / 180.0f;
        arrowImage.transform = CGAffineTransformMakeRotation(heading);
    }
}
```

❶ If location updates are also enabled, the location manager returns both true heading and magnetic heading values. If location updates are not enabled, or the location of the device is not yet known, the location manager returns only the magnetic heading value and the value returned by this call will be −1.

You're done: save your changes, and then click the Run button in the Xcode toolbar to deploy your new application onto your device. If you hold your device in Face Up or Portrait mode, you should see something very similar to Figure 4-4.

Unfortunately, as it stands your application has a critical flaw. If the user orientates the device into Landscape Mode, the reported headings will be incorrect, or at least look incorrect to the user. This will become especially important when you look at augmented reality interfaces later in the book; such interfaces are generally viewed in Landscape Left mode.

Determining the Heading in Landscape Mode

The magnetic and true headings are correct when the iPhone device is held like a traditional compass. In portrait mode, if the user rotates the device, then the heading readings will still be in this frame of reference. Even though the user has not changed the direction he is facing, the heading values reported by the device will have changed. You're going to have to correct for orientation before reporting headings back to the user (see Figure 4-5).

In the Project navigator, click the *CompassViewController.xib* file to open it in Interface Builder, then drag and drop another `UILabel` from the Object Library in the Utility pane into the View window. While using the Assistant Editor, connect the label to a new outlet in the *CompassViewController.h* interface file, as in Figure 4-6.

Figure 4-4. The compass application running on the iPhone 3GS

After doing so, the interface file should look like the following:

```
@interface CompassViewController : UIViewController <CLLocationManagerDelegate> {

    IBOutlet UILabel *trueHeadingLabel;
    IBOutlet UILabel *magneticHeadingLabel;
    IBOutlet UILabel *orientationLabel;
    IBOutlet UIImageView *arrowImage;

}
```

Just as you did for the Accelerometer application in Chapter 3, you're going to use this to report the current device orientation.

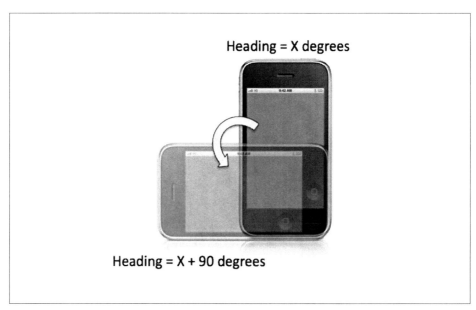

Figure 4-5. The real heading of the user when he is holding the device in landscape mode is the reported heading + 90 degrees

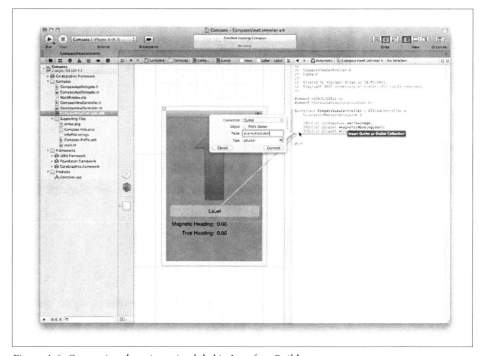

Figure 4-6. Connecting the orientation label in Interface Builder

---

Close the Assistant Editor and reopen the *CompassViewController.h* interface file in the Standard Editor. Then, add the following convenience methods to the class definition:

```
- (float)magneticHeading:(float)heading
        fromOrientation:(UIDeviceOrientation) orientation;
- (float)trueHeading:(float)heading
        fromOrientation:(UIDeviceOrientation) orientation;
- (NSString *)stringFromOrientation:(UIDeviceOrientation) orientation;
```

Save your changes, and open the corresponding *CompassViewController.m* implementation file. Unfortunately, since the CLHeading object is read only, you can't modify it directly. Therefore, you're going to add the following method that will correct the magnetic heading for the device orientation:

```
-(float)magneticHeading:(float)heading
        fromOrientation:(UIDeviceOrientation) orientation {

    float realHeading = heading;
    switch (orientation) {❶
        case UIDeviceOrientationPortrait:
            break;
        case UIDeviceOrientationPortraitUpsideDown:
            realHeading = realHeading + 180.0f;
            break;
        case UIDeviceOrientationLandscapeLeft:
            realHeading = realHeading + 90.0f;
            break;
        case UIDeviceOrientationLandscapeRight:
            realHeading = realHeading - 90.0f;
            break;
        default:
            break;
    }
    while ( realHeading > 360.0f ) {
        realHeading = realHeading - 360;
    }
    return realHeading;
}
```

❶ The UIDeviceOrientationFaceUp and UIDeviceOrientationFaceDown orientation cases are undefined and the user is presumed to be holding the device in UIDeviceOrientationPortrait mode.

However, you will also need to add a corresponding method to correct the true heading.

```
-(float)trueHeading:(float)heading fromOrientation:(UIDeviceOrientation) orientation {

    float realHeading = heading;
    switch (orientation) {❶
        case UIDeviceOrientationPortrait:
            break;
        case UIDeviceOrientationPortraitUpsideDown:
            realHeading = realHeading + 180.0f;
            break;
        case UIDeviceOrientationLandscapeLeft:
```

```
                realHeading = realHeading + 90.0f;
                break;
        case UIDeviceOrientationLandscapeRight:
                realHeading = realHeading - 90.0f;
                break;
        default:
                break;
    }
    while ( realHeading > 360.0f ) {
            realHeading = realHeading - 360;
    }
    return realHeading;
}
```

❶ The UIDeviceOrientationFaceUp and UIDeviceOrientationFaceDown orientation cases are undefined and the user is presumed to be holding the device in UIDeviceOrientationPortrait mode.

Finally, add the stringFromOrientation: method from Chapter 5. You'll use this to update the orientationLabel outlet.

```
- (NSString *)stringFromOrientation:(UIDeviceOrientation) orientation {

    NSString *orientationString;
    switch (orientation) {
        case UIDeviceOrientationPortrait:
            orientationString =  @"Portrait";
            break;
        case UIDeviceOrientationPortraitUpsideDown:
            orientationString =  @"Portrait Upside Down";
            break;
        case UIDeviceOrientationLandscapeLeft:
            orientationString =  @"Landscape Left";
            break;
        case UIDeviceOrientationLandscapeRight:
            orientationString =  @"Landscape Right";
            break;
        case UIDeviceOrientationFaceUp:
            orientationString =  @"Face Up";
            break;
        case UIDeviceOrientationFaceDown:
            orientationString =  @"Face Down";
            break;
        case UIDeviceOrientationUnknown:
            orientationString = @"Unknown";
            break;
        default:
            orientationString = @"Not Known";
            break;
    }
    return orientationString;
}
```

When that's done, return to the locationManager:didUpdateHeading: delegate method and modify the lines highlighted below to use the new methods and update your headings depending on the device orientation.

```
- (void)locationManager:(CLLocationManager*)manager
        didUpdateHeading:(CLHeading*)newHeading {

    UIDevice *device = [UIDevice currentDevice];
    orientationLabel.text = [self stringFromOrientation:device.orientation];

    if (newHeading.headingAccuracy > 0) {
        float magneticHeading = [self magneticHeading:newHeading.magneticHeading
                                        fromOrientation:device.orientation];
        float trueHeading = [self trueHeading:newHeading.trueHeading
                                fromOrientation:device.orientation];

        magneticHeadingLabel.text = [NSString stringWithFormat:@"%f", magneticHeading];
        trueHeadingLabel.text = [NSString stringWithFormat:@"%f", trueHeading];

        float heading = -1.0f * M_PI * newHeading.magneticHeading / 180.0f;❶
        arrowImage.transform = CGAffineTransformMakeRotation(heading);
    }
}
```

❶ You should still use the directly reported newHeading.magneticHeading for the compass needle rather than the adjusted heading, otherwise the compass will not point correctly.

Make sure you've saved all the changes to the implementation file and click the Run button in the Xcode toolbar to deploy the application onto the device. If all goes well, you should see the same compass display as before. However, if you rotate the display this time, the heading values should be the same, irrespective of the device orientation (see Figure 4-7).

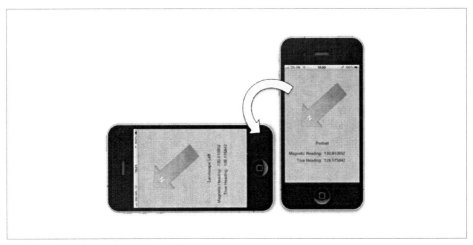

Figure 4-7. Heading values are now the same, irrespective of orientation

Although you have not implemented it here, if the CLLocationManager object encounters an error, it will call the locationManager:didFailWithError: delegate method.

```
- (void)locationManager:(CLLocationManager *)manager
      didFailWithError:(NSError *)error {
  if ([error code] == kCLErrorDenied) {
    // User has denied the application's request to use location services.
    [manager stopUpdatingHeading];

  } else if ([error code] == kCLErrorHeadingFailure) {
    // Heading could not be determined
  }
}
```

CHAPTER 5

Geocoding

If you were developing on a platform that didn't support geocoding, you'd need to make use of one of the many web services that provide geocoding (see later in this chapter for one such service). However, with the arrival of iOS 5, Apple has provided native support for both forward and reverse geocoding.

 Although reverse geocoding was provided in the Map Kit framework by the now deprecated `MKReverseGeocoder` class, before the arrival of iOS 5, there was no forward geocoding capabilities offered natively by the SDK. With the introduction of the `CLGeocoder` (*http://developer .apple.com/library/ios/documentation/CoreLocation/Reference/ CLGeocoder_class/Reference/Reference.html#//apple_ref/occ/cl/ CLGeocoder*) class, part of the Core Location framework, both capabilities are now natively provided. The `CLGeocoder` class should be used for all new application development.

Reverse Geocoding

 Both forward and reverse geocoding requests make a network connection back to web services hosted by Apple. The calls will fail without a network connection.

Reverse geocoding is the process of converting coordinates (latitude and longitude) into place name information. From iOS 5 you should use the `CLGeocoder` class to make reverse-geocoding requests by passing it a `CLLocation` object.

```
CLLocation *location =
    [[CLLocation alloc] initWithLatitude:37.323 longitude:-122.031];
CLGeocoder *geocoder = [[CLGeocoder alloc] init];

[geocoder reverseGeocodeLocation: location
    completionHandler: ^(NSArray *placemarks, NSError *error) {❶
```

```
        for (CLPlacemark *placemark in placemarks) {

            NSLog(@"Placemark is %@", placemark);

        }
    }];
```

❶ The completion handler block is called when the reverse geocoding request returns.

Using Alternative Reverse Geocoding Services

There are many web services that provide reverse geocoding. One of these is offered by the GeoNames.org (*http://www.geonames.org/*) site and it will return an XML or JSON document listing the nearest populated place using reverse geocoding. Requests to the service take this form (*http://ws.geonames.org/findNearbyPlaceName?lat=XX.X&lng= XX.X*) if you want an XML document returned, or this form (*http://ws.geonames.org/ findNearbyPlaceNameJSON?lat=XX.X&lng=XX.X*) if you prefer a JSON document. There are several optional parameters: **radius** (in km), **max** (maximum number of rows returned), and **style** (*SHORT*, *MEDIUM*, *LONG*, and *FULL*).

Passing the longitude and latitude of Cupertino, CA, the JSON service would return the following JSON document:

```
{
    "geonames":[
        {
            "countryName":"United States",
            "adminCode1":"CA",
            "fclName":"city, village,...",
            "countryCode":"US",
            "lng":-122.0321823,
            "fcodeName":"populated place",
            "distance":"0.9749",
            "fcl":"P",
            "name":"Cupertino",
            "fcode":"PPL",
            "geonameId":5341145,
            "lat":37.3229978,
            "population":50934,
            "adminName1":"California"
        }
    ]
}
```

Forward Geocoding

Forward geocoding is the process of converting place names into coordinates (latitude and longitude). From iOS 5 you can use the CLGeocoder class to make forward-geo-coding requests using either a dictionary of Address Book information (see Chapter 11) or an NSString. There is no designated format for string-based requests; delimiter characters are welcome, but not required, and the geocoding service treats the string as case-insensitive.

```
NSString *address = @"1 Infinite Loop, CA, USA";
CLGeocoder *geocoder = [[CLGeocoder alloc] init];

[geocoder geocodeAddressString:address
    completionHandler:^(NSArray* placemarks, NSError* error){ ❶

        for (CLPlacemark *placemark in placemarks) {

            NSLog(@"Placemark is %@", placemark);

        }
}];
```

❶ The completion handler block is called when the reverse geocoding request returns.

Building an Example App

Let's build a quick example application.

Open Xcode, choose Create a new Xcode project in the startup window, and then choose the Single View Application template from the iOS section of the New Project popup window. When prompted, name your new project *GeoCoder*. In the Company Identifier box, enter the root part of your Bundle Identifier used in your Provisioning Profile (see the iOS Provisioning Portal if you don't know it); for me, this is *uk.co.babilim*. You should leave the Class Prefix box blank and ensure that the Device Family is set to iPhone, with the checkbox for ARC ticked. The boxes for storyboard and unit tests should not be ticked. Save your project, and then when the Xcode project window opens, add the Core Location framework.

Click the project icon at the top of the Project pane in Xcode. Click the main Target for the project, and then click the Build Phases tab. Finally, click the Link Binary with Libraries item to open up the list of linked frameworks, and click the + symbol to add a new framework. Select the *CoreLocation.framework* from the drop-down list and click the Add button to add the framework to your project.

Now that you've imported the Core Location framework, let's build the user interface. Open up the *ViewController.xib* file and drag and drop five UILabel objects, three UITextField objects, and two UIButton objects into the view. Position them as in Figure 5-1.

Open the Assistant editor and right-click and drag the three UITextField objects into the View Controller code to create three IBOutlet properties. Call them latitude, longitude, and address, respectively. Then right-click and drag the two UIButton objects into the code and create an IBAction for each (see Figure 5-2). Call the methods rever seButton: and forwardButton:, respectively.

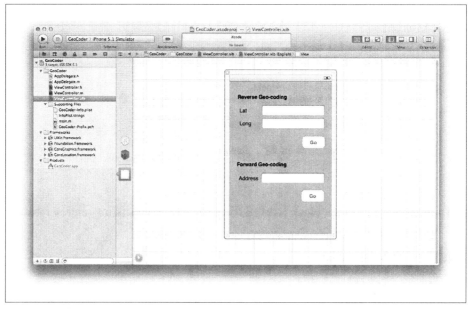

Figure 5-1. The user interface

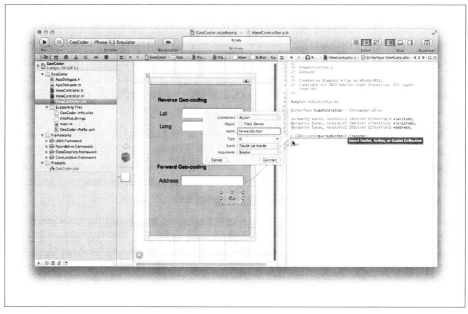

Figure 5-2. Connecting the outlets and actions to the view controller code

Next, right-click and drag each of the three UITextField objects to the File's Owner icon at the top of the Dock and connect them to the delegate outlet (see Figure 5-3).

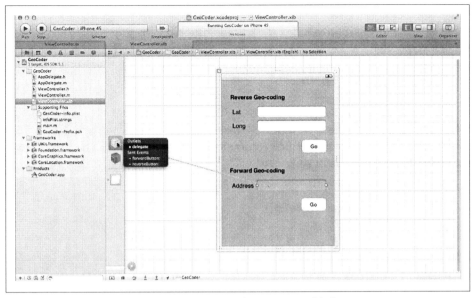

Figure 5-3. Make File's Owner the delegate of all three UITextField objects

Save your changes and close the Assistant editor. Click the *ViewController.h* interface file to open it in the Standard editor.

The `UITextFieldDelegate` protocol offers a rich set of delegate methods. To use them, you must declare your class as implementing that delegate protocol. So, declare that your view controller implements the protocol, and additionally declare an instance variable to point to whichever of your three `UITextField` objects is actively being edited by the user.

```
#import <UIKit/UIKit.h>

@interface ViewController : UIViewController <UITextFieldDelegate> {

    UITextField *activeTextField;❶
}

@property (weak, nonatomic) IBOutlet UITextField *latitude;
@property (weak, nonatomic) IBOutlet UITextField *longitude;
@property (weak, nonatomic) IBOutlet UITextField *address;

- (IBAction)reverseButton:(id)sender;
- (IBAction)forwardButton:(id)sender;

@end
```

❶ If your application has more than one text field in the view, it's useful to keep track of which is currently the active field by using an instance variable.

Save your changes and open the corresponding *ViewController.m* implementation file. When the user taps the text field, the `textFieldShouldBeginEditing:` method is called in the delegate to ascertain whether the text field should enter edit mode and become the first responder.

```
- (BOOL)textFieldShouldBeginEditing:(UITextField *)textField {
    activeTextField = textField;
    return YES;
}
```

When editing ends, the `textFieldShouldReturn:` method is called in the delegate. You can use this callback to resign as first responder, which will have the effect of making the keyboard disappear from your view.

```
- (BOOL)textFieldShouldReturn:(UITextField *)textField {
    activeTextField = nil;
    [textField resignFirstResponder];
    return YES;
}
```

Add both of these delegate callbacks to your code, and import the Core Location framework; we're going to need it.

```
#import <CoreLocation/CoreLocation.h>
```

Move to the `reverseButton:` method, and add the following code:

```
- (IBAction)reverseButton:(id)sender {

    CLLocation *location = [[CLLocation alloc]
                        initWithLatitude:[self.latitude.text doubleValue]
                            longitude:[self.longitude.text doubleValue]];

    NSLog(@"location = %@", location);
    CLGeocoder *geocoder = [[CLGeocoder alloc] init];

    [geocoder reverseGeocodeLocation: location
                completionHandler: ^(NSArray *placemarks, NSError *error) {

                    NSLog(@"completed");
                    if ( error ) {
                        NSLog(@"error = %@", error );
                        dispatch_async(dispatch_get_main_queue(),^{

                            UIAlertView *alert = [[UIAlertView alloc]
                                initWithTitle:@"Error"
                                message:[self errorMessage:error.code]
                                delegate:nil
                                cancelButtonTitle:nil
                                otherButtonTitles:@"OK", nil];
                            [alert show];
                            });
                    }
                    for (CLPlacemark *placemark in placemarks) {

                        NSLog(@"Placemark is %@", placemark);
```

```
                        UIAlertView *alert = [[UIAlertView alloc]
                            initWithTitle:@"Result"
                            message:[NSString stringWithFormat:@"%@",placemark]
                            delegate:nil
                            cancelButtonTitle:nil
                            otherButtonTitles:@"OK", nil];
                        [alert show];
                    }
                }];
    }

    - (NSString *)errorMessage:(int) code {❶

        NSString *message = nil;
        switch (code) {
            case kCLErrorLocationUnknown:
                message = @"Location Unknown";
                break;
            case kCLErrorDenied:
                message = @"Denied";
                break;
            case kCLErrorNetwork:
                message = @"Network Error";
                break;
            case kCLErrorGeocodeFoundNoResult:
                message = @"No Result Found";
                break;
            case kCLErrorGeocodeFoundPartialResult:
                message = @"Partial Result";
                break;
            case kCLErrorGeocodeCanceled:
                message = @"Cancelled";
                break;
            default:
                message = @"Unknown Error";
                break;
        }
        return message;

    }
```

❶ You're using the **errorMessage:** convenience method to generate a human readable string from the returned error code in those cases where you have an error.

This takes the latitude and longitude text fields and passes them to the geocoder, which then makes a network call to Apple to resolve to the nearest placemark (or possibly multiple placemarks).

Save your changes and click the Run button in the Xcode toolbar to build and deploy your application into the iPhone Simulator (or onto your device).

The iPhone Simulator can sometimes have problems doing geocoding requests. If you have problems, try deploying your code onto your device and testing it there.

If all goes well, you should see something like Figure 5-4. Enter a latitude and longitude (in decimal degrees) and tap on the "Go" button, and you should get a result back. This should occur almost instantly.

Figure 5-4. Your user interface (left), an example of successful reverse geocoding (center), and failed reverse geocoding (right)

Everything seems to be working, so let's finish up and implement forward geocoding. There's just one problem. Open up the application, either in the iPhone Simulator or on your device, and then tap on your third UITextField object. The keyboard will present itself, and cover the entry widget. That's not optimal, so let's fix that before proceeding.

Click the *ViewController.xib* file to open it in Interface Builder. For each of the three UITextField objects, open the Attributes Inspector in the Utility Panel and set the tag value. Set the latitude field to have a tag of 1, the longitude to have a tag of 2, and the address field to have a tag of 3 (see Figure 5-5).

You can use these tags in your code in order to tell the difference between the three text fields, and then move the main view appropriately so that the text field is no longer underneath the keyboard when it is presented. The obvious place to do this is from the text field delegate methods.

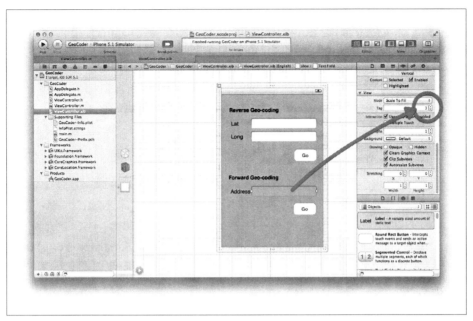

Figure 5-5. Setting the tag value of the third UITextField to 3

In the `textFieldShouldBeginEditing:` method, add the following code:

```
- (BOOL)textFieldShouldBeginEditing:(UITextField *)textField {
    activeTextField = textField;

    CGAffineTransform transform;
    switch (textField.tag) {
        case 1:
            transform = CGAffineTransformMakeTranslation(0,0);
            break;
        case 2:
            transform = CGAffineTransformMakeTranslation(0,-50);
            break;
        case 3:
            transform = CGAffineTransformMakeTranslation(0,-120);
            break;
        default:
            transform = CGAffineTransformMakeTranslation(0,0);
            break;
    }
    [UIView beginAnimations:@"MoveAnimation" context:nil];
    [UIView setAnimationCurve:UIViewAnimationCurveEaseInOut];
    [UIView setAnimationDuration:0.3];
    self.view.transform = transform;
    [UIView commitAnimations];

    return YES;
}
```

You can see that you translate the position of the main view by different amounts depending on which of the three text fields is the active text field. Then, in the text FieldShouldReturn: method, move the main view back to its original position:

```
- (BOOL)textFieldShouldReturn:(UITextField *)textField {
    activeTextField = nil;

    CGAffineTransform transform = CGAffineTransformMakeTranslation(0,0);
    [UIView beginAnimations:@"MoveAnimation" context:nil];
    [UIView setAnimationCurve:UIViewAnimationCurveEaseInOut];
    [UIView setAnimationDuration:0.3];
    self.view.transform = transform;
    [UIView commitAnimations];

    [textField resignFirstResponder];
    return YES;
}
```

Save your changes and deploy the application into the iPhone Simulator. You should see the behavior you're expecting, with the main view moving up and down depending on which of the text fields is selected (see Figure 5-6).

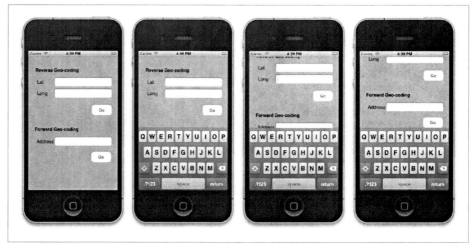

Figure 5-6. With no field selected (left), with the top field selected (center left), with the second field selected (center right), and with the final field selected (right)

Now that you've fixed that fairly serious bug in your user interface, you can implement the forwardButton: method. You can reuse the errorMessage: convenience method from earlier; the code looks a lot like the previous example, so there's not a lot to do here.

```
- (IBAction)forwardButton:(id)sender {

    NSString *place = self.address.text;
    CLGeocoder *geocoder = [[CLGeocoder alloc] init];
```

```
[geocoder geocodeAddressString:place
          completionHandler:^(NSArray* placemarks, NSError* error){

    NSLog(@"completed");
    if ( error ) {
        NSLog(@"error = %@", error );
        dispatch_async(dispatch_get_main_queue(),^{

            UIAlertView *alert = [[UIAlertView alloc]
                    initWithTitle:@"Error"
                          message:[self errorMessage:error.code]
                         delegate:nil
                cancelButtonTitle:nil
                otherButtonTitles:@"OK", nil];
            [alert show];

        });

    }
    for (CLPlacemark *placemark in placemarks) {

        NSLog(@"Placemark is %@", placemark);
        UIAlertView *alert = [[UIAlertView alloc]
                initWithTitle:@"Result"
                      message:[NSString stringWithFormat:@"%@", placemark]
                     delegate:nil
            cancelButtonTitle:nil
            otherButtonTitles:@"OK", nil];
        [alert show];

    }
}];

}
```

Save your changes and click the Run button to build and deploy your application. Enter an address in the address text field and hit the related Go button. If all goes well, you should see an alert view with the corresponding latitude and longitude (see Figure 5-7).

Figure 5-7. Successfully forward geocoding an address to a latitude and longitude

CLPlacemark Objects

Both forward and reverse geocoding requests return an array of CLPlacemark objects. While you've just dropped the placemark directly into your alert view, it's a fairly rich source of data. It stores data including information such as the country, state, city, and street address associated with the specified latitude and longitude coordinate, although it can also include points of interest and geographically-related data nearby.

Adding CLPlacemarks to Maps

While a CLPlacemark can't be immediately added to a map view, it's very easy to create a corresponding MKPlacemark annotation and add that to the map. For example:

```
MKPlacemark *mapPlacemark = [[MKPlacemark alloc] initWithPlacemark:placemark];
[self.mapView addAnnotation:mapPlacemark];
```

So, replace your alerts with a proper map.

 You'll need to add the Map Kit framework to your project in the same fashion as you added the Core Location framework earlier.

Then right-click the GeoCoder group in the Project Navigator panel and click New File from the menu. Under Cocoa Touch, select a `UIViewController` subclass, and name it **MapViewController** when prompted. Ensure the "With XIB for user interface" checkbox is ticked.

Let's start by creating the user interface for the new map view. Click the *MapView-Controller.xib* file to open the nib file in Interface Builder. Drag and drop a navigation bar (`UINavigationBar`) from Object Library, and position it at the top of the view. Then drag a map view (`MKMapView`) into the view and resize it to fill the remaining portion of the View window. Finally, drag a bar button item (`UIBarButton`) onto the navigation bar. In the Attributes Inspector tab of the Utility panel, change its identifier from Custom to Done. Once you're done this, your view will look similar to Figure 5-8.

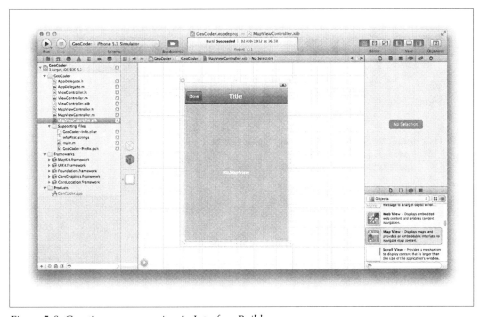

Figure 5-8. Creating your map view in Interface Builder

After saving the changes to the *MapViewController.xib* file, open the *MapViewController.h* interface file. Just as you did for the web view, you want to make this class self-contained so that you can reuse it without any modifications. You're therefore going to override the `init:` function to pass the information you need when instantiating the object:

```
#import <UIKit/UIKit.h>
#import <MapKit/MapKit.h>
#import <CoreLocation/CoreLocation.h>

@interface MapViewController : UIViewController <MKMapViewDelegate> {
    NSArray *mapAnnotations;
    IBOutlet MKMapView *mapView;
```

```
    IBOutlet UINavigationItem *mapTitle;
}

- (id) initWithPlacemarks:(NSArray *)placemarks;
- (IBAction) done:(id)sender;

@end
```

Do the same in the corresponding *MapViewController.m* implementation file:

```
#import "MapViewController.h"

@interface MapViewController ()

@end

@implementation MapViewController

- (id)initWithNibName:(NSString *)nibNameOrNil bundle:(NSBundle *)nibBundleOrNil {
    self = [super initWithNibName:nibNameOrNil bundle:nibBundleOrNil];
    if (self) {

    }
    return self;
}

- (id) initWithPlacemarks:(NSArray *)placemarks {
    if ( self = [super init] ) {
        mapAnnotations = placemarks;
    }
    return self;
}

- (IBAction) done:(id)sender {
    [self dismissModalViewControllerAnimated:YES];
}

- (void)viewDidLoad {
    [super viewDidLoad];
    for (CLPlacemark *placemark in mapAnnotations) {

        NSLog(@"Placemark is %@", placemark);
        MKPlacemark *mapPlacemark = [[MKPlacemark alloc]
            initWithPlacemark:placemark];
        [mapView addAnnotation:mapPlacemark];

    }

}

- (void)viewDidUnload {
    [super viewDidUnload];
}

- (BOOL)shouldAutorotateToInterfaceOrientation:
        (UIInterfaceOrientation)interfaceOrientation {
```

```
        return (interfaceOrientation == UIInterfaceOrientationPortrait);
}

@end
```

Save your changes and click the *MapViewController.xib* nib file to open it in Interface
Builder. Right-click and drag from File's Owner to the title item in the navigation bar
and connect it to the `mapTitle` outlet. Similarly, right-click and drag from File's Owner
to the map view to connect it to the `mapView` outlet. Finally, right-click and drag from
the Done button to File's Owner and connect it to the `done:` received action (see Figure 5-9) and from the map view to File's Owner to connect it as a delegate.

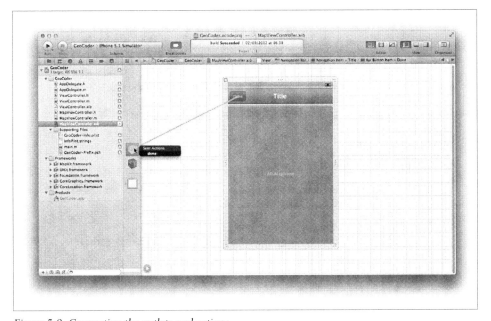

Figure 5-9. Connecting the outlets and actions

Save your changes to the nib file and switch to the *ViewController.m* implementation
file, then import the `MapViewController` class:

```
#import "MapViewController.h"
```

Then replace the code inside the `reverseButton:` and `forwardButton:` methods as below:

```
- (IBAction)reverseButton:(id)sender {

    CLLocation *location =
        [[CLLocation alloc] initWithLatitude:[self.latitude.text doubleValue]
            longitude:[self.longitude.text doubleValue]];

    NSLog(@"location = %@", location);
    CLGeocoder *geocoder = [[CLGeocoder alloc] init];
```

```
        [geocoder reverseGeocodeLocation: location
                completionHandler: ^(NSArray *placemarks, NSError *error) {

                NSLog(@"completed");
                if ( error ) {
                    NSLog(@"error = %@", error );
                    dispatch_async(dispatch_get_main_queue(),^{

                        UIAlertView *alert = [[UIAlertView alloc]
                            initWithTitle:@"Error" message:
                                [self errorMessage:error.code]
                            delegate:nil
                            cancelButtonTitle:nil
                            otherButtonTitles:@"OK", nil];
                        [alert show];

                    });

                }
                MapViewController *mapView = [[MapViewController alloc]
                    initWithPlacemarks:placemarks];
                [self presentModalViewController:mapView animated:YES];
            }];
}

- (IBAction)forwardButton:(id)sender {

    NSString *place = self.address.text;
    CLGeocoder *geocoder = [[CLGeocoder alloc] init];

    [geocoder geocodeAddressString:place
            completionHandler:^(NSArray* placemarks, NSError* error){

        NSLog(@"completed");
        if ( error ) {
            NSLog(@"error = %@", error );
            dispatch_async(dispatch_get_main_queue(),^{

                UIAlertView *alert =
                    [[UIAlertView alloc] initWithTitle:@"Error"
                        message:[self errorMessage:error.code]
                        delegate:nil
                        cancelButtonTitle:nil
                        otherButtonTitles:@"OK", nil];
                [alert show];

            });
        }
        MapViewController *mapView = [[MapViewController alloc]
            initWithPlacemarks:placemarks];
        [self presentModalViewController:mapView animated:YES];
    }];
}
```

Save your changes and click the Run button in the Xcode tool bar to build and deploy your application. You should see something very much like Figure 5-10.

Figure 5-10. Entering an address to forward geocode (left) and the resulting annotated map (right)

You can slightly improve on that, however. Go back to your `viewDidLoad:` method inside your *MapViewController.m* implementation and pull out the first item in the placemark array.

```
- (void)viewDidLoad {
    [super viewDidLoad];
    for (CLPlacemark *placemark in mapAnnotations) {

        NSLog(@"Placemark is %@", placemark);
        MKPlacemark *mapPlacemark = [[MKPlacemark alloc]
            initWithPlacemark:placemark];
        [mapView addAnnotation:mapPlacemark];

    }

    CLPlacemark *first = (CLPlacemark *)[mapAnnotations objectAtIndex:0];
    MKCoordinateRegion region = { first.location.coordinate , {0.2, 0.2} };

    mapTitle.title = first.locality;
    [mapView setRegion:region animated:NO];

}
```

Now if you build and deploy the application again, you'll get something like Figure 5-11.

Figure 5-11. Entering an address to forward geocode (left), the resulting annotated map (center), and the annotation information (right)

CHAPTER 6

Drawing Heat Maps

One of the more obvious missing features of the Map Kit framework is the ability to render heat maps on top of map views. However, while you've only met polygon overlays so far (see Chapter 3), it is also possible to use the overlay images on top of maps. You can use that to draw heat maps on top of your maps that will be fixed in the map view and move around as the user scrolls the map back and forth.

 The demonstration application we're going to build in this chapter makes heavy use of heat map code written by George Polak at Skyhook Wireless. Thanks to him and the all the team at Skyhook Wireless (*http://www.skyhookwireless.com*), both for the code and assistance. The SHGeoUtils class is copyright Skyhook Wireless and used with permission; it is distributed under an MIT license.

Building an Earthquake Map

You're going to build a demonstration application with a heat map from data representing the Richter scale magnitude of a recent earthquake in New England.

Open Xcode and choose Create a new Xcode project in the startup window. Choose the Single View Application template from the iOS section of the New Project popup window. When prompted, name your new project **HeatMap**. In the Company Identifier box, enter the root part of your Bundle Identifier (see the iOS Provisioning Portal) used in your Provisioning Profile; for me, this is *uk.co.babilim*. You should leave the Class Prefix box blank. Ensure that the Device Family is set to iPhone, the checkbox for ARC is ticked, and the boxes for storyboard and unit tests are not ticked.

Save your project. When the Xcode project window opens, add the Map Kit and Core Location frameworks.

Click the project icon at the top of the Project pane in Xcode, click the main Target for the project, and then click the Build Phases tab. Finally, click the Link Binary with Libraries item to open up the list of linked frameworks, and click the + symbol to add a new framework. Select the *MapKit.framework* from the drop-down list and click the Add button to add the framework to your project. Then select the *CoreLocation.framework* from the list and similarly add it to your project.

Now that you've imported the Map Kit and Core Location frameworks, click the Supporting Files group in the Project navigator, and then click the *Location_Prefix.pch* file to open it in the standard editor. Instead of having to include the framework every time you need it, you can use this header file to import it into all the source files in the project, as highlighted in bold below:

```
#ifdef __OBJC__
    #import <Foundation/Foundation.h>
    #import  <UIKit/UIKit.h>
    #import  <CoreLocation/CoreLocation.h>
    #import  <MapKit/MapKit.h>
#endif
```

This file is prefixed to all of your source files. However, the compiler precompiles it separately; this means it does not have to reparse the file on each compile run, which can dramatically speed up your compile times on larger projects.

Adding Earthquake Data

To keep things simple, you're going to provide the earthquake data as a *.plist* file inside your application bundle and pass that to the code that will generate the overlay image. You can of course use your own data if you like, but the data I'm using here is available for download; if you can't be bothered, you should just grab that.

 You can download the earthquake data I'm using directly from the book's website (*http://programmingiphonesensors.com/data/Earth Quake-Data.plist*).

If you look inside the *.plist* file, you'll see something that looks like this:

```
<?xml version="1.0" encoding="UTF-8"?>
<!DOCTYPE plist PUBLIC "-//Apple//DTD PLIST 1.0//EN"
                       "http://www.apple.com/DTDs/PropertyList-1.0.dtd">
<plist version="1.0">
<array>
    <dict>
            <key>magnitude</key>
        <real>3.4</real>
        <key>latitude</key>
        <real>42.7409</real>
        <key>longitude</key>
        <real>-71.4587</real>
    </dict>
    <dict>
        <key>magnitude</key>
```

```
            <real>2</real>
            <key>latitude</key>
            <real>41.7387</real>
            <key>longitude</key>
            <real>-72.6697</real>
        </dict>
        <dict>
            <key>magnitude</key>
            <real>2</real>
            <key>latitude</key>
            <real>41.3384</real>
            <key>longitude</key>
            <real>-72.6265</real>
        </dict>
            .
            .
            .
    </array>
    </plist>
```

If you haven't come across one before, a *.plist* file is often used to store a user's settings, but it's also used to store information and configuration data for applications, as you're doing here.

In any case, drag and drop the data file into your project into the Supporting Files group in the Project Navigator. If you click it afterwards, you should see something like Figure 6-1.

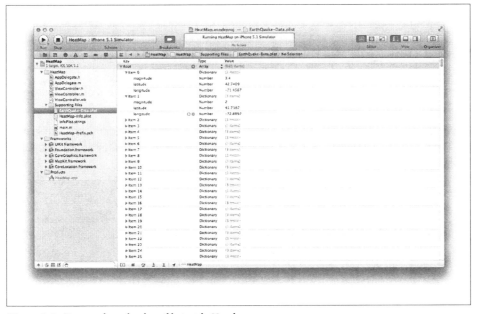

Figure 6-1. Our earthquake data file inside Xcode

Building the User Interface

Now click the *ViewController.xib* nib file to open the Interface Builder. Open up the Utility panel and drag and drop a Map View (`MKMapView`) from the Object Library into your view. Then close the Utility panel, open the Assistant editor, and right-click and drag from the map view to your header file to connect the view to your code as an `IBOutlet` (see Figure 6-2).

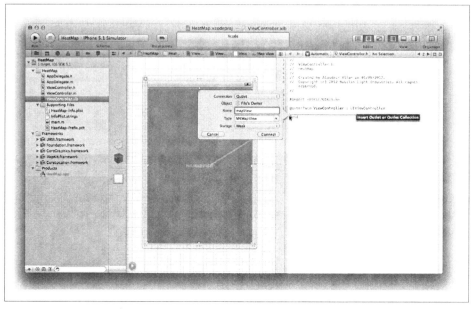

Figure 6-2. Connecting the Map View to the View Controller header file

Then right-click and drag from the Map View to the App Delegate icon at the top of the dock to make the View Controller a delegate of our new Map View (see Figure 6-3).

Once you've done that, close the Assistant editor and reopen the Standard editor, and click the *ViewController.h* interface file. Declare the View Controller as an `MKMapView Delegate` as part of the interface declaration:

```
#import <UIKit/UIKit.h>

@interface ViewController : UIViewController <MKMapViewDelegate>

@property (weak, nonatomic) IBOutlet MKMapView *mapView;

@end
```

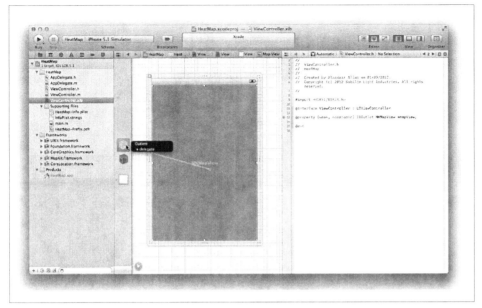

Figure 6-3. Making the View Controller a Map View delegate

By clicking the corresponding implementation file, you need to initialize your map view in the `viewDidLoad:` method:

```
- (void)viewDidLoad {
    [super viewDidLoad];

    MKCoordinateSpan span = MKCoordinateSpanMake(10.0, 13.0);
    CLLocationCoordinate2D center = CLLocationCoordinate2DMake(39.0, -77.0);
    MKCoordinateRegion region = MKCoordinateRegionMake(center, span);
    self.mapView.region = region;

}
```

Once you save your changes and click the Run button in the Xcode toolbar, you'll see that the map will be centered somewhere around Washington D.C. (see Figure 6-4).

At this point, similar to the polygon-style overlays you saw in Chapter 3, you need to create an object that implements the `MKOverlay` protocol and a corresponding `MKOverlay View` object. However, since your image overlays are going to be slightly more involved than the polygons you used last time, you're going to have to roll your own implementations of these classes.

Adding the Overlay

Right-click on the HeatMap group in the Project Navigator, select New file from the menu, choose an Objective-C class, and make the new class a subclass of `NSObject` and class it **MapOverlay** when prompted.

Figure 6-4. Our Map View in the iPhone Simulator

Do this again, but this time you should create your new class as a subclass of the MKOverlayView class rather than NSObject. Name this class **MapOverlayView** when prompted to do so.

You should end up with four new files; *MapOverlay.h*, *MapOverlay.m*, *MapOverlayView.h*, and *MapOverlayView.m*.

Click the *MapOverlay.h* interface file to open it in the Standard editor, declare that it implements the MKOverlay protocol, and change it as follows:

```
#import <Foundation/Foundation.h>

@interface MapOverlay : NSObject <MKOverlay> {
    CLLocationCoordinate2D _coordinate;
    MKMapRect _mapRect;
    MKMapView *_mapView;
}

- (id)initWithView:(MKMapView *)mapView;
- (MKMapRect)boundingMapRect;

@property (nonatomic, readonly) CLLocationCoordinate2D coordinate;
@property (nonatomic, readonly) MKMapRect mapRect;
@property (nonatomic, strong) MKMapView *mapView;

@end
```

Change it in the corresponding *MapOverlay.m* implementation file as well:

```
#import "MapOverlay.h"

@implementation MapOverlay

@synthesize mapView=_mapView;

- (id)initWithView:(MKMapView *)mapView {
    if (self = [super init]) {
        self.mapView = mapView;
        _coordinate = mapView.centerCoordinate;
        _mapRect = mapView.visibleMapRect;
    }
    return self;
}

-(CLLocationCoordinate2D)coordinate {
    return _coordinate;
}

- (MKMapRect)boundingMapRect {
    return _mapRect;
}

@end
```

You can see that you're going to pass the Map View you want to put the overlay on top of to your overlay class, and use that map view to configure the center and boundaries of your overlay.

 You should notice that you're extracting the center and boundaries of the Map View when you initially create the overlay. If you do not do this, then the resulting overlay will not scale correctly as the map view is zoomed in and out.

Essentially you're going to overlap an image over your entire Map View, or at least the part that is initially visible in the Window when your application starts up.

You can leave the *MapOverlayView.h* interface file as it is—you don't need to make any changes there. Instead, open the *MapOverlayView.m* implementation file and add the required drawMapRect:zoomScale:inContext: method.

```
#import "MapOverlayView.h"
#import "MapOverlay.h"

@implementation MapOverlayView

- (void)drawMapRect:(MKMapRect)mapRect zoomScale:(MKZoomScale)zoomScale
                                  inContext:(CGContextRef)ctx {

    // Load in earthquake data
    NSString *dataFile = [[NSBundle mainBundle] pathForResource:@"EarthQuake-Data"
```

```
                                                    ofType:@"plist"];
NSArray *quakeData = [[NSArray alloc] initWithContentsOfFile:dataFile];

NSMutableArray *locations =
    [[NSMutableArray alloc] initWithCapacity:[quakeData count]];
NSMutableArray *weights =
    [[NSMutableArray alloc] initWithCapacity:[quakeData count]];

for (NSDictionary *reading in quakeData) {
    CLLocationDegrees latitude =
        [[reading objectForKey:@"latitude"] doubleValue];
    CLLocationDegrees longitude =
        [[reading objectForKey:@"longitude"] doubleValue];
    double magnitude = [[reading objectForKey:@"magnitude"] doubleValue];

    CLLocation *location =
        [[CLLocation alloc] initWithLatitude:latitude longitude:longitude];
    [locations addObject:location];
    [weights addObject:[NSNumber numberWithInteger:(magnitude * 10)]];
}

//Loading and set up the image overlay
MKMapRect theMapRect = [self.overlay boundingMapRect];
CGRect theCGRect = [self rectForMapRect:theMapRect];

MapOverlay *overlay = (MapOverlay *)self.overlay;
MKMapView *view = overlay.mapView;

UIImage *heatmap = nil; // ... insert code here to generate the heatmap ...
CGImageRef imageRef = heatmap.CGImage;

// Flip and reposition the image
CGContextScaleCTM(ctx, 1.0, -1.0);
CGContextTranslateCTM(ctx, 0.0, -theCGRect.size.height);

//drawing the image to the context
CGContextDrawImage(ctx, theCGRect, imageRef);
}

@end
```

Go back to the *ViewController.m* implementation file and import both your new classes:

```
#import "MapOverlay.h"
#import "MapOverlayView.h"
```

Then do the same in the viewDidLoad: method:

```
- (void)viewDidLoad {
    [super viewDidLoad];

    MKCoordinateSpan span = MKCoordinateSpanMake(10.0, 13.0);
    CLLocationCoordinate2D center = CLLocationCoordinate2DMake(39.0, -77.0);
    MKCoordinateRegion region = MKCoordinateRegionMake(center, span);
    self.mapView.region = region;
```

```
    MapOverlay * mapOverlay = [[MapOverlay alloc] initWithView:self.mapView];
    [self.mapView addOverlay:mapOverlay];

}
```

Create your overlay. Finally, you need to add the delegate callback to the same class:

```
- (MKOverlayView *)mapView:(MKMapView *)mapView
          viewForOverlay:(id <MKOverlay>)overlay {

    MapOverlay *mapOverlay = (MapOverlay *)overlay;
    MapOverlayView *mapOverlayView =
        [[MapOverlayView alloc] initWithOverlay:mapOverlay];

    return mapOverlayView;
}
```

If you save your changes and click the Run button in the Xcode toolbar, your application should successfully build and deploy into the iPhone Simulator. Of course, this happens right at the moment the overlaid image is set to nil, so the application will look exactly the same as it did in Figure 6-4, but you should be able to check that everything builds and runs correctly.

Adding the Heat Map

Let's fix that right now. To do that, you're going to make use of the SHGeoUtils class, written by George Polak of Skyhook Wireless.

 You can download the SHGeoUtils class files from the book's website at:

http://programmingiphonesensors.com/code/SHGeoUtils.h

http://programmingiphonesensors.com/code/SHGeoUtils.m

The code is released under an MIT license.

Looking at the SHGeoUtils class, you can see that it provides three class methods. All of them will return a UIImage that can then be used by your MapOverlayView class.

```
#import <Foundation/Foundation.h>

@interface SHGeoUtils : NSObject

+ (UIImage *)heatMapForMapView:(MKMapView *)mapView
        boost:(float)boost
        locations:(NSArray *)locations
        weights:(NSArray *)weights;❶

+ (UIImage *)heatMapWithRect:(CGRect)rect
        boost:(float)boost
        points:(NSArray *)points
        weights:(NSArray *)weights;❷
```

```
+ (UIImage *)heatMapWithRect:(CGRect)rect
        boost:(float)boost
        points:(NSArray *)points
        weights:(NSArray *)weights
        weightsAdjustmentEnabled:(BOOL)weightsAdjustmentEnabled
        groupingEnabled:(BOOL)groupingEnabled;❸

@end
```

❶ This generates a heat map image for the specified map view. You pass the locations as an **NSArray** of **CLLocation** objects and the weights as an **NSArray** of **NSNumber** objects corresponding to the weighting of each point. There should be a one-to-one correspondence between the location and weight elements. Passing a **nil** weight parameter implies an even weight distribution between the location points. The boost value represents a radius multiplier: values close to 1.0 will produce very diffuse maps, while values close to 0.0 will produce maps that are pointlike in nature.

❷ Instead of specifiying a map view, you are asked to specifiy a **CGRect** region frame for the view and your locations as an **NSArray** of **NSValue CGPoint** objects representing the data points.

❸ The final method allows you to adjust the weighting of the points you pass to the heat map code: setting **YES** allows weight balancing and normalization to occur. You can also enable grouping: setting **YES** allows for tighter visual grouping of dense areas of data.

Download the utility classes and drag and drop them into your project.

You've set up your overlay view so that you can easily use the first—and most convenient—of the three methods provided by the **SHGeoUtils** class. Click the *MapOverlay-View.m* implementation file to open it in the editor, and in the **drawMapRect:zoom Scale:inContext:** method, make the following change:

```
- (void)drawMapRect:(MKMapRect)mapRect zoomScale:(MKZoomScale)zoomScale
                           inContext:(CGContextRef)ctx {

    // Load in earthquake data
    NSString *dataFile =
        [[NSBundle mainBundle] pathForResource:@"EarthQuake-Data" ofType:@"plist"];
    NSArray *quakeData = [[NSArray alloc] initWithContentsOfFile:dataFile];

    NSMutableArray *locations =
        [[NSMutableArray alloc] initWithCapacity:[quakeData count]];
    NSMutableArray *weights =
        [[NSMutableArray alloc] initWithCapacity:[quakeData count]];

    for (NSDictionary *reading in quakeData) {
        CLLocationDegrees latitude =
            [[reading objectForKey:@"latitude"] doubleValue];
        CLLocationDegrees longitude =
            [[reading objectForKey:@"longitude"] doubleValue];
        double magnitude =
```

```
        [[reading objectForKey:@"magnitude"] doubleValue];

    CLLocation *location =
        [[CLLocation alloc] initWithLatitude:latitude longitude:longitude];
    [locations addObject:location];
    [weights addObject:[NSNumber numberWithInteger:(magnitude * 10)]];
}

//Loading and set up the image overlay
MKMapRect theMapRect = [self.overlay boundingMapRect];
CGRect theCGRect = [self rectForMapRect:theMapRect];

MapOverlay *overlay = (MapOverlay *)self.overlay;
MKMapView *view = overlay.mapView;

UIImage *heatmap = [SHGeoUtils heatMapForMapView:view
                                           boost:0.67
                                       locations:locations
                                         weights:weights];
CGImageRef imageRef = heatmap.CGImage;

// Flip and reposition the image
CGContextScaleCTM(ctx, 1.0, -1.0);
CGContextTranslateCTM(ctx, 0.0, -theCGRect.size.height);

//drawing the image to the context
CGContextDrawImage(ctx, theCGRect, imageRef);
}
```

Save your changes and click the Run button in the Xcode editor. If all goes well, you should see something like Figure 6-5.

Figure 6-5. Your map with a heat map of the earthquake data overlaid on top (center), zoomed out (left), and zoomed in (right)

At this point, you should be able to pan the map as normal, rotate the interface into landscape mode and back, and pinch and zoom. The heat map should move and scale, just as you'd expect.

Overlaying Other Data

At this point, you can generalize your MapOverlay and MapOverlayView classes somewhat to cope with arbitrary data. For instance, you can modify your MapOverlay class to take both the locations and weights during initialization rather than reading these in inside your MapOverlayView class. Changing the *MapOverlay.h* interface file as below:

```
#import <Foundation/Foundation.h>
#import <MapKit/MapKit.h>

@interface MapOverlay : NSObject <MKOverlay> {
    CLLocationCoordinate2D _coordinate;
    MKMapRect _mapRect;
    MKMapView *_mapView;
    NSArray *_locations;
    NSArray *_weights;
}

- (MKMapRect)boundingMapRect;

- (id)initWithView:(MKMapView *)mapView
      andLocations:(NSArray *)locations
        andWeights:(NSArray *)weights;


@property (nonatomic, readonly) CLLocationCoordinate2D coordinate;
@property (nonatomic, readonly) MKMapRect mapRect;
@property (nonatomic, strong) MKMapView *mapView;
@property (nonatomic, strong) NSArray *locations;
@property (nonatomic, strong) NSArray *weights;

@end
```

along with the *MapOverlay.m* implementation

```
#import "MapOverlay.h"

@implementation MapOverlay

@synthesize mapView=_mapView;
@synthesize locations=_locations;
@synthesize weights=_weights;

- (id)initWithView:(MKMapView *)mapView
      andLocations:(NSArray *)locations
        andWeights:(NSArray *)weights {
    if (self = [super init]) {
        self.mapView = mapView;
        self.locations = locations;
        self.weights = weights;
```

```
        _coordinate = mapView.centerCoordinate;
        _mapRect = mapView.visibleMapRect;

    }
    return self;
}

-(CLLocationCoordinate2D)coordinate {
    return _coordinate;
}

- (MKMapRect)boundingMapRect {
    return _mapRect;
}

@end
```

allows us to modify the *MapOverlayView.m* implementation.

```
#import "MapOverlayView.h"
#import "MapOverlay.h"
#import "SHGeoUtils.h"

@implementation MapOverlayView

- (void)drawMapRect:(MKMapRect)mapRect
          zoomScale:(MKZoomScale)zoomScale
          inContext:(CGContextRef)ctx {

    //Loading and setting the image
    MKMapRect theMapRect = [self.overlay boundingMapRect];
    CGRect theCGRect = [self rectForMapRect:theMapRect];

    MapOverlay *overlay = (MapOverlay *)self.overlay;
    MKMapView *view = overlay.mapView;

    UIImage *heatmap = [SHGeoUtils heatMapForMapView:view
                                               boost:0.67
                                           locations:overlay.locations
                                             weights:overlay.weights];
    CGImageRef imageRef = heatmap.CGImage;

    // We need to flip and reposition the image here
    CGContextScaleCTM(ctx, 1.0, -1.0);
    CGContextTranslateCTM(ctx, 0, -theCGRect.size.height);

    //drawing the image to the context
    CGContextDrawImage(ctx, theCGRect, imageRef);
}

@end
```

Overlaying Other Types of Images

You might have noticed that your call to the heat map code hooks into your overlay code in just one place, so your code can be easily modified to display any image. If you drag and drop an image of an American flag into your project and edit the `drawMap Rect:zoomScale:inContext:` method in the `MapOverlayView` implementation to pull that image instead of your earthquake data heat map, you get something like Figure 6-6 when you build and run the new code.

Figure 6-6. A zoomed-out view of the image overlay.

For example:

```
- (void)drawMapRect:(MKMapRect)mapRect
         zoomScale:(MKZoomScale)zoomScale
         inContext:(CGContextRef)ctx {

    //Loading and setup the image
    MKMapRect theMapRect = [self.overlay boundingMapRect];
    CGRect theCGRect = [self rectForMapRect:theMapRect];

    UIImage *image  = [UIImage imageNamed:@"Flag.png"];
    CGImageRef imageRef = heatmap.CGImage;
```

```
    // We need to flip and reposition the image here
    CGContextScaleCTM(ctx, 1.0, -1.0);
    CGContextTranslateCTM(ctx, 0.0, -theCGRect.size.height);

    //drawing the image to the context
    CGContextDrawImage(ctx, theCGRect, imageRef);
}
```

The size of the flag denotes the size of the extent of the original map view as your current overlay code scales the size of the overlaid object to be the size of the existing map view on startup.

CHAPTER 7

Further Information and Third-Party SDKs

Almost done. I've covered most of the information you'll need to get started writing geobased applications for the iPhone, iPad, and iPod touch. However, there is a lot of great third-party software available and you shouldn't spend your time reinventing the wheel. If you're thinking about adding advanced geocapabilities to your application, you should probably look at some of the third-party SDKs and libraries before rolling your own implementation.

Skyhook Wireless

Skyhook Wireless were the first people to develop a commercial software-only location system based on WiFi positioning, GPS, and cell tower triangulation, and when the iPhone first launched, it shipped and used their backend for WiFi positioning. Apple later replaced Skyhook's database with in-house data. However, the company still remains a force in the field.

SpotRank

Skyhook's SpotRank service is unique at the time of writing (as far as I know). It can offer predictions on the density of people in a specified area worldwide at any hour and on any day of the week. Predictions are at the US-block level and based on the company's years of positioning data from real devices doing position fixes to determine their location (see Figure 7-1).

More information about SpotRank, and a link to request a demonstration of the service, can be found here (*http://www.skyhookwireless.com/location-intelligence/*).

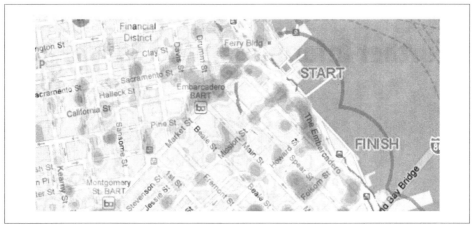

Figure 7-1. Representative data from SkyHook Wireless' SpotRank service for San Francisco

Local Faves

Skyhook also offers its Local Faves SDK that allows you to add location-aware features (like tagging and check-ins) and social features (like sharing and raking) into your application fairly painlessly. You'll need to sign up for a developer account to download and use the SDK, and more information is available here (*https://www.skyhookwireless .com/localfaves/*).

GeoLoqi

GeoLoqi is a location startup based in Portland that has an interesting platform based around real-time location tracking and geofenced carrier agnostics messaging backed by their own hosted spatial cloud storage platform.

The easiest way to get started with their SDK is to download their sample application; they've got a good guide here (*https://developers.geoloqi.com/ios/getting-started*), which will walk you through not just getting the sample application up and running (see Figure 7-2), but also integrating the SDK into your own application.

You'll need an API key to get the sample app up and running. You can register for a free account (*https://developers.geoloqi.com/account/plans/signup?plan_id=egg*), which will allow you access to the developer site and the ability to register new applications.

MapBox

If you want to add custom maps to your application, then you might want to look at the MapBox SDK. Among other things, it offers the ability to custom design your own maps, add layers on top of OpenStreetMap data, and display them embedded in your applications while the user is in both online and offline mode. You'll need an account

Figure 7-2. The GeoLoqi sample application running in the iPhone Simulator

to get started; more information about their SDK and hosting services is available here (*http://mapbox.com*). An example application is available on GitHub (*https://git hub.com/mapbox/mapbox-ios-example*) (see Figure 7-3).

Bing Maps Control for iOS

If you'd like to use Microsoft's Bing Maps in place of the native maps provided by the Map Kit framework, Microsoft has provided a native control to allow you to embed their Bing Maps directly into your application, in almost exactly the same fashion as the native Map Kit objects.

Similarly, the Bing Maps Control for iOS provides support for adding placemarks and other overlays to the map, allows the device's location to be displayed, and provides some geocoding methods.

The Bing Maps Control for iOS can be downloaded from Microsoft (*http://www.micro soft.com/en-us/download/details.aspx?id=1112*). The SDK comes with several example applications. Figure 7-4 shows the LocationMap sample application running on my iPad.

Figure 7-3. The MapBox example application running in the iPhone Simulator

You'll need a Bing Maps Developer Account, which in turn requires a Microsoft Account. You can sign up for both of these here (*https://www.bingmapsportal.com/*). From there, you'll need to create an API key, which you can do from the "Create or view keys" item under My Account.

Unlike most other third-party SDKs for iOS, you'll need to add the Bing Maps API key to your main project *Info.plist* file rather than placing it inline inside your code.

While the Bing Maps credentials provided by Microsoft's portal work fine when your applications are deployed to the device, it seems they do not work in the iPhone or iPad Simulators. If your application is running in the Simulator, it will complain about invalid credentials even if they work when the application is running on the device.

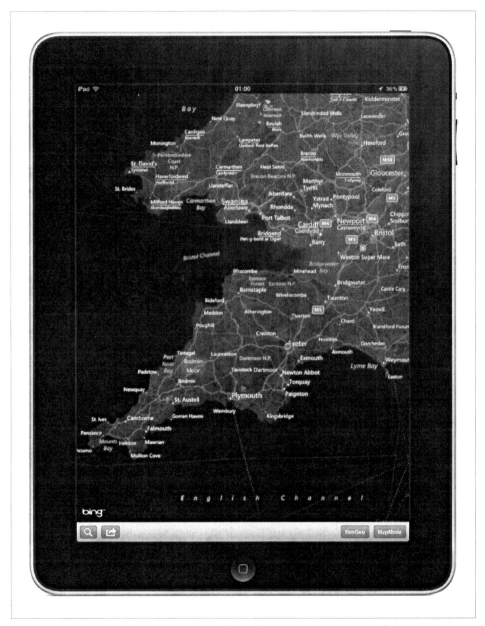

Figure 7-4. The Microsoft LocationMap sample application running on my iPad

ArcGIS for iOS

If you're an old school GIS person, you'll be familiar with ESRI and ArcGIS, and you'll probably want to take a look at their iOS SDK. It allows you to embed ArcGIS maps and tasks into your application and use services provided by ArcGIS Online and ArcGIS Server. More information about the runtime is available here (*http://resources.arcgis.com/en/communities/runtime-ios-sdk/*).

Urban Airship

Known for push notifications and in-app purchasing, the Portland startup also offers a geofenced push notification service known as Segments (*http://urbanairship.com/products/segments/*).

Foursquare

While there isn't an official Foursquare SDK, there are at least two well-supported iOS client libraries for the Foursquare v2 API available on GitHub. Among them, I'd probably recommend *https://github.com/baztokyo/foursquare-ios-api* as being one of the better documented libraries.

About the Author

Alasdair Allan is the author of *Learning iOS Programming*, *iOS Sensor Programming*, *Basic Sensors in iOS*, *Geolocation in iOS*, *iOS Sensor Apps with Arduino*, and *Augmented Reality in iOS* (all by O'Reilly). Last year he and Pete Warden caused a privacy scandal by uncovering that iPhones record a user's location at all times—this caused several class action lawsuits and a US Senate hearing. From time to time he stands in front of cameras, and you can often find him at conferences run by O'Reilly Media.

He runs a small technology consulting business writing bespoke software, building open hardware, and providing training, including a series of workshops on sensors. He sporadically writes blog posts about things that interest him, or more frequently provides commentary about them in 140 characters or less.

Alasdair is also a senior research fellow at the University of Exeter. As part of his work there he built a distributed peer-to-peer network of telescopes, which, acting autonomously, reactively scheduled observations of time-critical events. Notable successes included contributing to the detection of the most distant object yet discovered, a gamma-ray burster at a redshift of 8.2.

Colophon

The animal on the cover of *Geolocation in iOS* is the brindled gnu.

The cover image is from *The Riverside Natural History*. The cover font is Adobe ITC Garamond. The text font is Linotype Birka; the heading font is Adobe Myriad Condensed; and the code font is LucasFont's TheSansMonoCondensed.

Get even more for your money.

Join the O'Reilly Community, and register the O'Reilly books you own. It's free, and you'll get:

- $4.99 ebook upgrade offer
- 40% upgrade offer on O'Reilly print books
- Membership discounts on books and events
- Free lifetime updates to ebooks and videos
- Multiple ebook formats, DRM FREE
- Participation in the O'Reilly community
- Newsletters
- Account management
- 100% Satisfaction Guarantee

Signing up is easy:

1. **Go to: oreilly.com/go/register**
2. **Create an O'Reilly login.**
3. **Provide your address.**
4. **Register your books.**

Note: English-language books only

To order books online:
oreilly.com/store

For questions about products or an order:
orders@oreilly.com

To sign up to get topic-specific email announcements and/or news about upcoming books, conferences, special offers, and new technologies:
elists@oreilly.com

For technical questions about book content:
booktech@oreilly.com

To submit new book proposals to our editors:
proposals@oreilly.com

O'Reilly books are available in multiple DRM-free ebook formats. For more information:
oreilly.com/ebooks

Spreading the knowledge of innovators   **oreilly.com**

Have it your way.

O'Reilly eBooks

- Lifetime access to the book when you buy through oreilly.com
- Provided in up to four DRM-free file formats, for use on the devices of your choice: PDF, .epub, Kindle-compatible .mobi, and Android .apk
- Fully searchable, with copy-and-paste and print functionality
- Alerts when files are updated with corrections and additions

oreilly.com/ebooks/

Safari Books Online

- Access the contents and quickly search over 7000 books on technology, business, and certification guides
- Learn from expert video tutorials, and explore thousands of hours of video on technology and design topics
- Download whole books or chapters in PDF format, at no extra cost, to print or read on the go
- Get early access to books as they're being **written**
- Interact directly with authors of upcoming books
- Save up to 35% on O'Reilly print books

See the complete Safari Library at safari.oreilly.com